WEDDING CAKES
OF DISTINCTION

INCLUDING SIDE DESIGN TEMPLATES

dutton

PUBLISHING

PUBLISHING

First published in the UK in March 2001 by b. Dutton Publishing Limited,

Alfred House, Hones Business Park, Farnham, Surrey, GU9 8BB.

Publisher: Beverley Dutton

Editor: Jenny Stewart

Design: Sarah Richardson

Photography: Alister Thorpe

Printed in Spain

CONTENTS

Sugar Flowers

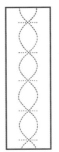

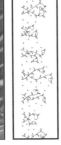

52-53 Rosalie

54-55 Gwen

72-73 Valentine

74-75 Tiffany

56-57 Clarissa

58-59 Marie

76-77 Brittany

78-79 Lacey

60-61 Rowena

62-63 Paige

80-81 Geena

82-83 Molly

64-65 Fern

66-67 Tabitha

84-85 Pandora

86-87 Hazel

68-69 Gabriella

70-71 Whitney

SILK FLOWERS

90-91 Silvia

92-93 Bryony

94-95 Tegan

96-97 Candis

114-115 Bernadette

116 Marcia

98-99 Sheena

100-101 Hollywood Rose

117 Nadia

102 Edith

103 Shelby

CHOCOLATE CAKES

120 Bronwen

121 Chrissie

FRESH FLOWERS

106-107 Ursula

107-108 Nadine

122-123 Bernice

124 Carla

110-111 Niamh

112-113 Amy

125 Dominique

126 Emily

127 TEMPLATES

128 SUPPLIERS

Cakes of Distinction by Linda Wolfe

Finest quality wedding and celebration cakes made to order. Nationwide delivery service.
Cakes of Distinction, Southwinds, Oakhanger, Bordon, Hampshire, GU35 9JN.
Tel: +44 (0)1420 473522 Fax: +44 (0)1420 473544
www.cakesofdistinction.com

Squires Group

Squires Kitchen Magazine Publishing Ltd.
Squires Kitchen International School of Cake Decorating & Sugarcraft
Squires Kitchen Sugarcraft
b. Dutton Publishing Ltd.

International sugarcraft specialists, manufacturers and distributors of cake decorating equipment and edibles. Shop,
school, worldwide mail order, and book and magazine publishers.
Squires House, 3 Waverley Lane, Farnham, Surrey, GU9 8BB.
Tel: +44 (0)1252 711749 Fax: +44 (0)1252 714714
www.squires-group.co.uk

Constance Spry

Leading florist and provider of leisure and professional flower arranging and floristry courses.
Constance Spry, Moor Park House, Moor Park Lane, Farnham, Surrey, GU9 8EN.
Tel: +44 (0)1252 734477 Fax: +44 (0)1252 712011
www.constancespry.com

Acknowledgements

The author would like to thank the following talented sugarcrafters for their flower making skills: Joyce Barton,
Alison Swayne, Christine Coombes, and Jacquie Elliot, with special thanks to the late Peggie Green for her
wonderful work as Linda's first tutor.

The publishers would like to thank Martine and Robert Frost, Fred Wilkinson and Dorothy Robinson at Constance
Spry for the stunning fresh flower sprays used on Linda's cakes; Joan Mooney at Great Impressions for the leaf
veiners; Alister Thorpe at Alister Thorpe Photography for his exceptional photographic skills (and his generous
assistance in cake tasting sessions!); the editor Jenny Stewart and designer Sarah Richardson for their
professionalism, cheerful good humour and brilliant teamwork.

INTRODUCTION

Having been a busy mum for a number of years, I did not enter the world of sugarcraft until the youngest of my four daughters started school in 1987. I spotted a course at Squires Kitchen's International School of Cake Decorating and, since then, have never looked back! Six months later, after completing a range of courses, I decided to start my own cake making business, Cakes of Distinction.

With much of my inspiration owing to my love of embroidery, crochet and flowers, the success of the business grew rapidly and has continued to do so since those early days. The smiles of joy and tears of happiness from clients when they view their cakes makes all the hard work and effort worthwhile. Today, I am proud to say that my mother and four daughters work alongside me in various aspects of the business, while my ever patient husband offers continuous support.

This, my first book, has been created for the many cake decorators who have approached me over the years and asked for templates of my side designs. It is also a source of inspiration for those who share my passion for flowers, with every design outlining my own personal choice of sprays (or other forms of decoration). I hope that you will find, as I have done, that creating intricate yet simple designs can give tremendous satisfaction and that this book will inspire you to create your own masterpieces in sugar.

Linda Wolfe.

Linda Wolfe

This book is dedicated to my husband, Michael, my daughters, Suzanna, Joanna, Lucy and Cloe, and my mother, Joyce, for their patience and support.

How To Use This Book

Within the pages of this book, you will find over fifty cake designs, each complete with a list of the materials required, alongside a full colour photograph of the finished cake. Where side designs are required, templates are given which can then be traced and transferred to the cake. (Please read A Guide to Using the Side Design Templates on pages 12-13.)

With each design, the cake boards and drums required are both given under the heading 'Boards'. Unless a drum is specified, a thin cake board should be used, for example, if the requirement list specifies '20cm (8") Round', a thin round board is required. Always remember that stacked cakes require boards between each tier, even if they cannot be seen.

Cake and board sizes and weights of materials (e.g. sugarpaste and marzipan) are given in both metric and imperial (rounded to the nearest unit). You will find a full list of the flowers and other decoration, as well as the colours used and special equipment needed (all Squires Kitchen products are prefixed by SK). I have made use of various inexpensive, non-edible decorations in a number of my designs, for example, beads, berries, ornamental wood, and fabric, which can be found in craft markets and haberdashery stores. It is recommended that non-edible items are placed on plaques which are easily removed before cutting the cake.

Although the majority of the cakes are standard shapes on standard-shaped boards, some designs suit more unusual shapes (for example, Ingrid, pages 50-51). Where this is the case, cakes can be cut to shape with a sharp knife, while boards can be cut to shape at a DIY store (or by a helpful husband!).

Cake Tins

Cake tins are a major investment for the serious cake decorator, but it is well worth the extra expense of purchasing good quality, heavy duty deep cake tins with a fixed base. If you are not planning to make large quantities of cakes, you may wish to hire stainless steel tins from your local sugarcraft shop. Accurate lining, with either greaseproof paper or re-usable lining sheets, is time well spent, giving neat edges to a baked cake. Always use separate pieces of greaseproof paper to line the bottom and sides, ensuring there are no gaps at the join.

Food Colourings

Food colourings come in four main forms: powder (or 'dust'), liquid, paste, and pens. Paste colours should be used to colour sugarpaste, marzipan and royal icing where dark shades are required. Liquids or pastes can be used for pastel shades and for painting onto icing. Powder colours are most commonly used to dust sugar flowers, but can also be used to colour white chocolate. For a greater colour intensity when using powder colours, lightly brush the surface with Gildesol before applying the colour. This method is also useful when colouring plaster pillars.

Flower Paste

When making sugar flowers, I use a ready-made commercial paste. However, if you wish to make your own flower paste, a number of recipes are widely available.

Sugarpaste and Marzipan

Although there are many recipes for homemade sugarpaste and marzipan, commercial pastes are extremely good and convenient to use. The quality of marzipans will vary with the proportion of almonds to sugar - in most cases, the higher the almond content, the better the quality of (and usually the more expensive) the marzipan.

Demerara sugarpaste is made from pure cane sugar and has a delicious and distinctive flavour. Its colour is stunning and works well in many designs, as well as being ideal where darker colours are to be added to paste. (For suppliers of demerara sugarpaste, see page 128.)

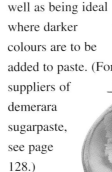

Chocolate Marzipan

Chocolate marzipan is a delicious undercoat for chocolate cakes and is simple to make in white, milk or dark chocolate flavour. Simply knead a quantity of SK Cocoform (made from couverture chocolate) until soft and pliable, then knead it together with the same amount of marzipan until the two are blended. Roll out the paste and cover the cake in the usual way.

Chocolate

I always use high quality couverture chocolate for my cakes. Although this will usually require tempering, it is worth the extra time involved to produce a cake with exceptional flavour. (Couverture chocolate does not need to be tempered if it is being used in ganache or for folding into buttercream.) Remember that chocolate cakes should be made close to the date required and should be stored in a cool place once covered to prevent the chocolate from melting.

Cake Stands

Cake stands can be purchased or hired from your local sugarcraft supplier. You will find a choice of many designs and materials, from traditional-style silverware to acrylic, chrome and plastic. The popular 'E' and 'S' chrome stands are a modern method of displaying the tiers of a cake without using pillars.

Silver Separators

Silver separators are an exclusive alternative to pillars. For supplier see page 128.

Cake Knives

Silver plated cake knives are available in a number of different pattern designs to hire or purchase from your local sugarcraft shop.

Pillars

Pillars are available in an enormous range of shapes, heights and designs, from plaster and plastic to acrylic and silver. When choosing pillars, it is important to remember that they should be an integral part of the cake design, as well as support for cake tiers. Plaster pillars can be coloured (if using dust colours, first apply a layer of Gildesol to adhere the colour to the pillar) or decorated with royal icing or ribbons.

Moulds

Silicone moulds made from food grade rubber are a brilliant time-saver for the commercial cake decorator, with many leaf veining designs, lace and figure moulds available.

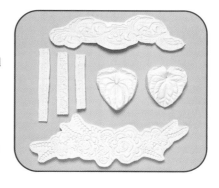

Cake Size	Round	Square	Hexagon	Octagon	Heart	Petal	Oval
15cm (6")	51cm	63cm	48cm	50cm	51cm	51cm	61cm
18cm (7")	59cm	74cm	56cm	57cm	58cm	60cm	69cm
20cm (8")	67cm	84cm	64cm	64cm	64cm	68cm	77cm
23cm (9")	75cm	94cm	72cm	74cm	74cm	74cm	85cm
25cm (10")	83cm	104cm	80cm	81cm	81cm	83cm	93cm
28cm (11")	91cm	114cm	88cm	89cm	89cm	89cm	100cm
30cm (12")	99cm	123cm	96cm	98cm	98cm	99cm	108cm
33cm (13")	107cm	134cm	104cm	112cm	112cm	106cm	116cm
36cm (14")	115cm	145cm	112cm	122cm	122cm	113cm	124cm
38cm (15")	123cm	155cm	120cm	127cm	127cm	122cm	132cm
40cm (16")	131cm	164cm	128cm	135cm	135cm	128cm	140cm

Ribbon Requirements

This table (left) is a guide to how much ribbon is required for board edging (given in cm). The figures include a 2cm overlap.

Ribbon Spacing

Although the majority of the cake designs in this book include piped side designs, an alternative means of side decoration is to use ribbon. Double ribbons in particular can create a stylish yet uncomplicated look if spaced correctly. To ensure that ribbons are attached at the same depth around a cake, hold a clean 30cm (12") ruler against the side of the cake and score a line on the icing along the top edge of the ruler. (The width of a standard ruler normally gives an ideal height for the highest ribbon.) To mark an even line at a different height, use spacers to score a line on the icing: my general rule is to leave 5mm ($^1/_4$") between each ribbon. Finally, remember that ribbons must be attached to each individual tier before they are stacked.

Sprays

The flowers, leaves and berries used on cakes should complement the design and not overpower it. I have included my personal choice of sprays (or alternative decoration) with my designs, but do use artistic licence and adapt designs to suit your requirements. Similarly, if you are recreating one of the 'Sugar Flower' designs but have a limited timescale, silk or fresh flowers can be used instead.

How Many Portions?

When deciding on the size of a wedding cake, it is best to overestimate the number of portions required. Always remember to wipe the knife blade between each cut to create neat slices. These charts are a guide to the number of slices you would expect to cut from various cake sizes.

RICH FRUIT CAKE				
Shape	15cm (6")	20cm (8")	25cm (10")	30cm (12")
Round	36	61	93	131
Square	36	64	100	144
Oval	20	40	58	86
Scalloped Oval	22	34	58	82
Petal	30	48	79	117
Hexagonal	24	42	66	90
Heart	26	46	74	104
Diamond		30	58	96

SOFT CAKES (Madeira, Sponge, etc)				
Shape	15cm (6")	20cm (8")	25cm (10")	30cm (12")
Round	16	33	53	72
Square	18	32	50	72
Oval	10	20	29	44
Scalloped Oval	10	18	30	44
Petal	14	22	45	65
Hexagonal	12	22	34	46
Heart	14	24	36	52
Diamond		20	36	52

A Guide to Using the Side Design Templates

The side design templates throughout the book are intended to be used as a guide, and are open to the artistic creativity of the cake designer. Always feel free to adjust or make additions to templates to suit your own (or you customer's) requirements. You will find that, in order to transfer the patterns onto the sides of every tier, a certain amount of adjusting will be required, as explained below. It may be useful, therefore, to keep a complete set of templates for each cake for future reference.

The first stage of transferring the side design template to your own cake is to trace the template on the page onto tracing paper. You will need to continue the repeating pattern until it is long enough to fit the circumference of the largest cake. (Always remember that, in order to accurately measure the circumference of a cake for a side design, it should already be covered.) Repeat the process on separate pieces of tracing paper so that you have a complete set of templates for all tiers before you start work on your cake. This allows you to measure the design against the cake before applying it and avoids unneccessary frustration at a later stage. Once you have a set of finished templates, hold each one up to the side of the relevant cake and mark out the pattern by gently pricking into the icing with a scriber tool. Once you have marked out the pattern on all the cakes, pipe/attach/emboss the pattern following your own guidelines.

In some cases, the same template can be repeated on all tiers (e.g. Isabelle, page 34). This type of template is the easiest to use and you may find that the template 'fits' exactly on each tier. However, once cakes have been covered, you may find that the pattern on the given template does not match up. If this is the case, there are two remedies.

1. Once you have traced the template for the specific tier you are working on, place it around the cake. If it is too short and does not have an exact fit, fill the gap by elongating the last two or three repeats of the pattern. Although this method involves a little freehand work, if you measure the space that needs to be filled with a piece of tracing paper, then fold it into two or three, you can adjust the pattern accordingly. This adjusted pattern can then be added on to the existing pattern for a seamless join.

2. Once you have traced the template, you may find that is is only slightly too short for the cake. If you do not wish to opt for the adjusting method, simply leave a gap which can then be covered up with an appropriately placed spray. If neccessary, pipe a few dots or swirls at the bottom of the tier to fill any space not covered by the flowers.

Many of the templates will need to be lengthened or shortened according to the size of the tier. For example, a scalloped pattern may be repeated six times around each tier, so the higher the tier (i.e. the smaller the cake), the shorter the repeating pattern will have to be. Where this is the case, a simple method can be used:

Using a separate piece of tracing paper for each tier, measure the circumference of each cake. If the pattern is to be repeated six times around each tier, fold each piece of paper into six equal sections, and, using the given template as a guide, draw the pattern onto one of the sections. Repeat this for each section (you may want to re-trace the first section each time to ensure they are all the same) and for each separate template, make a final check against the cake to ensure an exact fit. You can then begin to scribe the pattern onto the icing. An important point to remember is that, when you are lengthening or shortening patterns in this way, as long as the depth of the tiers remains constant, so must the depth of the template. For example, if the depth of the curve in a scallop is 2.5cm (1"), this should remain constant. It is wise to mark the lowest point of a scallop in the centre of each section first, then continue the curve up to each corner.

In some cases, where space allows, individual templates for each tier have been printed. Where this is the case, the hard work has been done for you and you should be able to simply transfer each template to your cake. However, it is always best to check that the templates are the correct size by holding them up to your cake before marking the design out on the icing.

Points to Remember

Always ensure you have a completed design for each tier drawn on tracing paper before starting any work on the cake and hold each design against the cake to be certain that it will fit exactly.

Use the given template and the photographs as a guide. Use your own judgement to make any necessary adjustments or changes - after all, each and every cake is an individual work of art.

Keep your templates for future reference, but remember that, even if two cakes are baked in the same size tin, their circumferences may well differ once they have been covered.

SUGAR FLOWERS

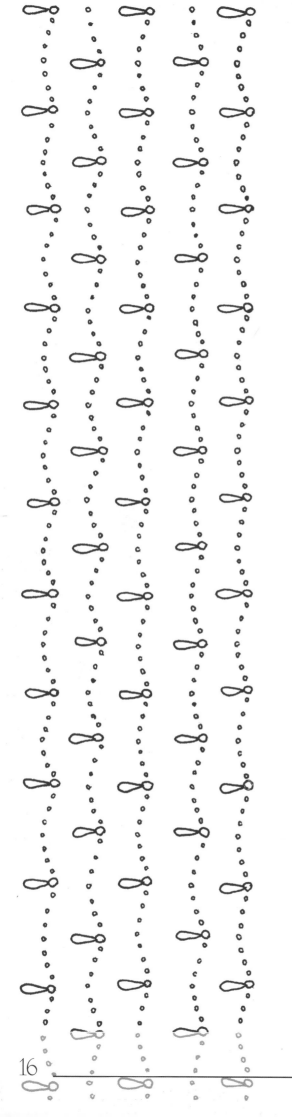

LOUISE

REQUIREMENTS

Flowers/Leaves

Top Tier

9 ivory roses and 3 ivory rose buds set against eucalyptus sprays, lilac Freesia sprays, and long ivy leaf sprays

Middle Tier

3 sprays each comprising 2 ivory roses, 3 ivory rose buds, eucalyptus sprays, lilac Freesia sprays, and long ivy leaf sprays

Bottom Tier

3 sprays each comprising 2 ivory roses, 3 ivory rose buds, eucalyptus sprays, Freesia sprays, and long ivy leaf sprays

Cake

Top Tier: 15cm (6") Hexagonal

Middle Tier: 20cm (8") Hexagonal

Bottom Tier: 25cm (10") Hexagonal

Middle Tier: 800g ($1^3/_4$lb)

Bottom Tier: 1.02kg ($2^1/_4$lb)

Royal Icing

White

Boards

Top Tier: 20cm (8") Hexagonal drum

Middle Tier: 25cm (10") Hexagonal drum

Bottom Tier: 36cm (14") Hexagonal drum

Ribbons

15mm white, 3mm white

Marzipan

Top Tier: 500g (1lb 1oz)

Middle Tier: 800g ($1^3/_4$lb)

Bottom Tier: 1.02kg ($2^1/_4$lb)

Pillars/Separators

6 x SK Barley Twist Pillars: White

Piping Nozzles

No. 1

Sugarpaste

Colour: White

Top Tier: 500g (1lb 1oz)

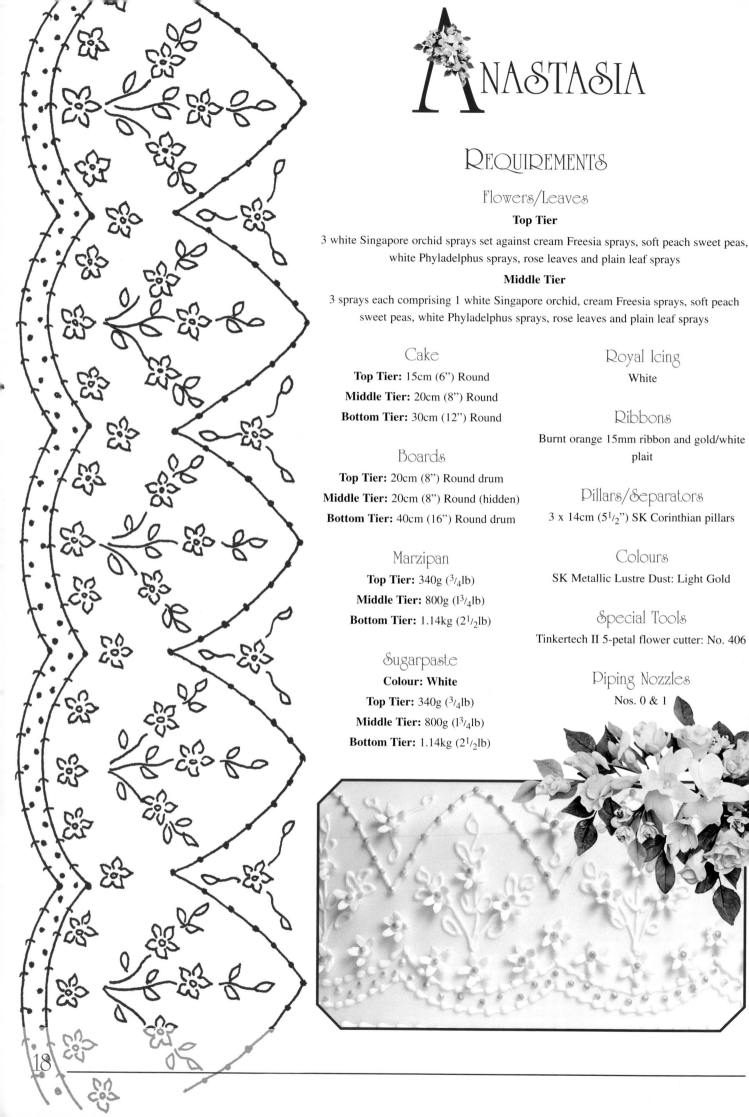

ANASTASIA

REQUIREMENTS

Flowers/Leaves

Top Tier

3 white Singapore orchid sprays set against cream Freesia sprays, soft peach sweet peas, white Phyladelphus sprays, rose leaves and plain leaf sprays

Middle Tier

3 sprays each comprising 1 white Singapore orchid, cream Freesia sprays, soft peach sweet peas, white Phyladelphus sprays, rose leaves and plain leaf sprays

Cake

Top Tier: 15cm (6") Round

Middle Tier: 20cm (8") Round

Bottom Tier: 30cm (12") Round

Boards

Top Tier: 20cm (8") Round drum

Middle Tier: 20cm (8") Round (hidden)

Bottom Tier: 40cm (16") Round drum

Marzipan

Top Tier: 340g ($^3/_4$lb)

Middle Tier: 800g (l$^3/_4$lb)

Bottom Tier: 1.14kg (2$^1/_2$lb)

Sugarpaste

Colour: White

Top Tier: 340g ($^3/_4$lb)

Middle Tier: 800g (l$^3/_4$lb)

Bottom Tier: 1.14kg (2$^1/_2$lb)

Royal Icing

White

Ribbons

Burnt orange 15mm ribbon and gold/white plait

Pillars/Separators

3 x 14cm (5$^1/_2$") SK Corinthian pillars

Colours

SK Metallic Lustre Dust: Light Gold

Special Tools

Tinkertech II 5-petal flower cutter: No. 406

Piping Nozzles

Nos. 0 & 1

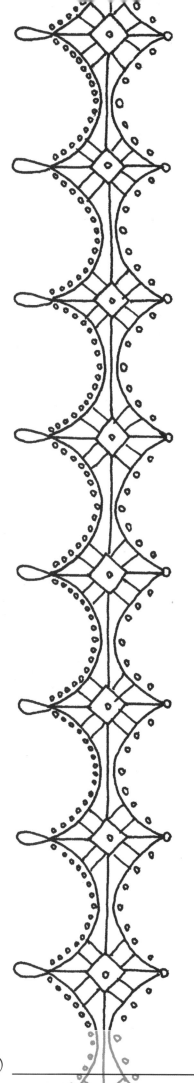

AVANNA

REQUIREMENTS

Flowers/Leaves

Top Tier

7 sprays of sweet peas in ivory, ivory with peach edges, peach, and orange set against ivy leaf sprays

Middle Tier

12 sprays of sweet peas in ivory, ivory with peach edges, peach, and orange set against ivy leaf sprays

Bottom Tier

16 sprays of sweet peas in ivory, ivory with peach edges, peach, and orange set against ivy leaf sprays

Cake

Top Tier: 20cm (8") Oval

Middle Tier: 25cm (10") Oval

Bottom Tier: 30cm (12") Oval

Boards

Top Tier: 25cm (10") Oval drum

Middle Tier: 30cm (12") Oval drum

Bottom Tier: 40cm (16") Oval drum

Marzipan

Top Tier: 570g (1¼lb)

Middle Tier: 950g (2lb 1oz)

Bottom Tier: 1.14kg (2½lb)

Sugarpaste

Colour: Peach

Top Tier: 570g (1¼lb)

Middle Tier: 950g (2lb 1oz)

Bottom Tier: 1.14kg (2½lb)

Royal Icing

Ivory coloured

Ribbons

15mm orange ribbon and bead braid

Pillars/Separators

3 tier chrome 'E' stand

Colours

SK Paste Food Colour: Nasturtium

SK Dust Food Colours: Berberis (use a hint to give ivory), shades of peach

Piping Nozzles

No. 1

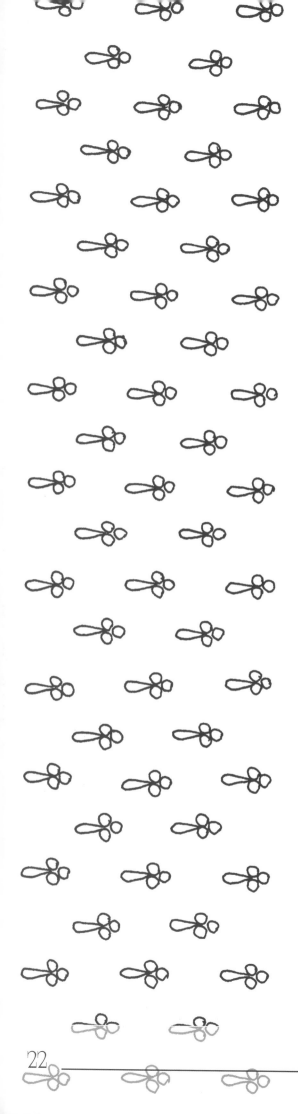

LAVINIA

REQUIREMENTS

Flowers/Leaves

Top Tier

3 large pink arum lilies with 2 arum lily leaves

Middle Tier

5 large pink arum lilies with 3 arum lily leaves

Bottom Tier

7 large pink arum lilies with 3 arum lily leaves

Cake

TopTier: 20cm (8") Diamond

Middle Tier: 25cm (10") Diamond

Bottom Tier: 30cm (12") Diamond

Boards

TopTier: 25cm (10") Diamond drum

Middle Tier: 30cm (12") Diamond drum

Bottom Tier: 40cm (16") Diamond drum

Marzipan

TopTier: 800g (1^3/$_4$lb)

Middle Tier: 1.02kg (2^1/$_4$lb)

Bottom Tier: 1.25kg (2^3/$_4$lb)

Sugarpaste

Demerara

TopTier: 800g (1^3/$_4$lb)

Middle Tier: 1.02kg (2^1/$_4$lb)

Bottom Tier: 1.25kg (2^3/$_4$lb)

Royal Icing

Demerara

Ribbons

15mm pink ribbon and 9mm gold plait

Pillars/Separators

3-tier chrome step stand

Colours

SK Metallic Lustre Dust: Light Gold

SK Bridal Satin Lustre Dust: Damask Rose

Piping Nozzles

No. 1

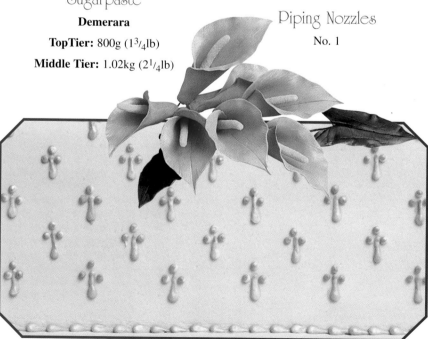

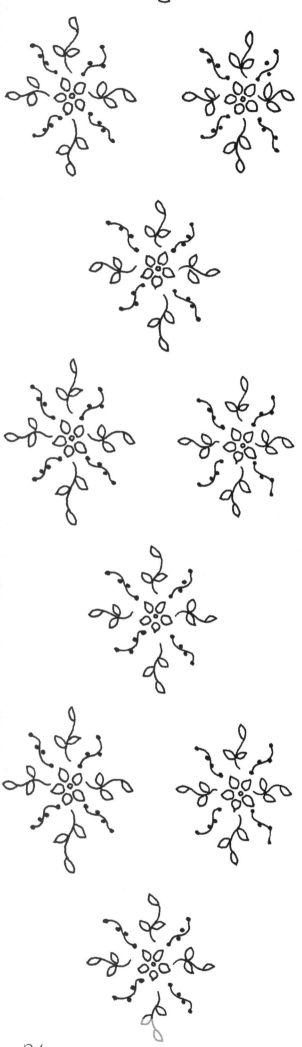

LAUREN

Requirements

Flowers/Leaves

Top Tier

3 white orchids set against 3 pale pink rose sprays, 3 bowed orchid leaves, 3 orchid leaves, sprays of variegated plain leaves and sprigs of Gypsophila

Upper Middle Tier

3 sprays each comprising 1 white orchid, 2 pale pink roses, 1 bowed orchid leaf, 1 orchid leaf, variegated plain leaves and sprigs of Gypsophila

Lower Middle Tier

3 sprays each comprising 2 white orchids, 3 pale pink roses, 1 bowed orchid leaf, 2 orchid leaves, variegated plain leaves and sprigs of Gypsophila

Bottom Tier

3 sprays each comprising 2 white orchids, 3 pale pink roses, 2 bowed orchid leaves, 2 orchid leaves, variegated plain leaves and sprigs of Gypsophila

Cake

Top Tier: 15cm (6") Round
Middle Top: 20cm (8") Round
Middle Bottom: 25cm (10") Round
Bottom Tier: 30cm (12") Round

Boards

Top Tier: 20cm (8") Round
Middle Top: 25cm (10") Round drum
Middle Bottom: 30cm (12") Round drum
Bottom Tier: 40cm (16") Round drum

Marzipan

Top Tier: 340g ($^3/_4$lb)
Upper Middle Tier: 570g (1$^1/_4$lb)
Lower Middle Tier: 950g (2lb 1oz)
Bottom Tier: 1.14kg (2$^1/_2$lb)

Sugarpaste

Colour: White

Top Tier: 340g ($^3/_4$lb)
Upper Middle Tier: 570g (1$^1/_4$lb)
Lower Middle Tier: 950g (2lb 1oz)
Bottom Tier: 1.14kg (2$^1/_2$lb)

Royal Icing

White

Ribbons

15mm white ribbon and lace overlay

Pillars/Separators

9 x 12cm (4 $^3/_4$") SK Barley Twist Pillars: White

Piping Nozzles

Nos. 0 and 1

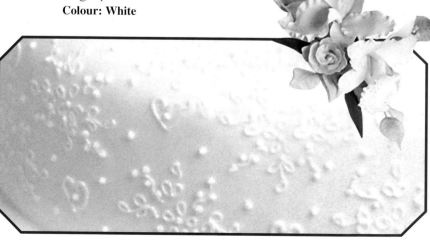

Juliana

Requirements

Flowers/Leaves

Top Tier

9 full and 9 half-open Christmas roses set against Christmas rose buds, gold berry clusters, and variegated ivy leaves

Middle Tier

3 sprays each comprising 2 medium Christmas roses, Christmas rose buds, gold berries, and medium and small variegated ivy leaves

Bottom Tier

3 sprays each comprising 2 large Christmas roses, Christmas rose buds, gold berries, and medium and small variegated ivy leaves

Base Board

3 sprays each comprising 2 large Christmas roses, 1 medium Christmas rose, gold berries, and medium and small variegated ivy leaves

Cake

Top Tier: 15cm (6") Hexagonal

Middle Tier: 23cm (9") Hexagonal

Bottom Tier: 30cm (12") Hexagonal

Boards

Top Tier: 15cm (6") Hexagonal (hidden)

Middle Tier: 23cm (9") Hexagonal (hidden)

Bottom Tier: 36cm (14") Hexagonal

Base Board: 40cm (16") Hexagonal drum

Marzipan

Top Tier: 500g (1lb 1oz)

Middle Tier: 950g (2lb 1oz)

Bottom Tier: 1.14kg ($2^1/_2$lb)

Sugarpaste

Demerara

Top Tier: 500g (1lb 1oz)

Middle Tier: 950g (2lb 1oz)

Bottom Tier: 1.14kg ($2^1/_2$lb)

Royal Icing

Demerara

Ribbons

15mm gold ribbon, thin and thick white/gold braid

Piping Nozzles

No. 1

ABIGAIL

REQUIREMENTS

Flowers/Leaves

Top Tier

12 large purple arum lilies and 9 large ivory arum lilies set against dark and variegated ivy leaves

Cake

Top Tier: 15cm (6") Round
Middle Top: 20cm (8") Round
Middle Bottom: 25cm (10") Round
Bottom Tier: 30cm (12") Round

Boards

Top Tier: 20cm (8") Round drum
Middle Top: 25cm (10") Round drum
Middle Bottom: 30cm (12") Round drum
Bottom Tier: 38cm (15") Round drum

Marzipan

Top Tier: 340g ($^3/_4$lb)
Upper Middle Tier: 570g ($1^1/_4$lb)
Lower Middle Tier: 950g (2lb 1oz)
Bottom Tier: 1.14kg ($2^1/_2$lb)

Sugarpaste

Colour: Ivory
Top Tier: 340g ($^3/_4$lb)
Upper Middle Tier: 570g ($1^1/_4$lb)
Lower Middle Tier: 950g (2lb 1oz)
Bottom Tier: 1.14kg ($2^1/_2$lb)

Royal Icing

Purple and ivory coloured

Ribbons

15mm ivory

Pillars/Separators

3 x cake drums:
15cm (6"), 20cm (8") and 25cm (10")

Colours

SK Paste Food Colours: Violet mixed with Wisteria (to give purple), Berberis (use a hint to give ivory)

Piping Nozzles

No. 1

$\mathcal{F}$AITH

REQUIREMENTS

Flowers/Leaves

Top Tier

19 sprays of pale pink roses set against soft green rose leaves

Other Tiers

Individual sprays comprising pale pink roses and buds and soft green rose leaves

Cake

Top Tier: 15cm (6") Round

Middle Tier: 20cm (8") Round

Bottom Tier: 25cm (10") Round

Boards

Top Tier: 15cm (6") Round (hidden)

Middle Tier: 20cm (8") Round (hidden)

Bottom Tier: 36cm (14") Round drum

Marzipan

Top Tier: 340g (³/₄lb)

Middle Tier: 570g (1¹/₄lb)

Bottom Tier: 950g (2lb 1oz)

Sugarpaste

Colour: White

Top Tier: 340g (³/₄lb)

Middle Tier: 570g (1¹/₄lb)

Bottom Tier: 950g (2lb 1oz)

Royal Icing

White

Ribbons

3mm and 15mm pale pink

Piping Nozzles

No. 1

ASTRID

Requirements

Flowers/Leaves

Top Tier

6 orange arum lilies set against yellow roses and buds, purple sweet peas, autumnal beech leaves and rose leaves

Middle Tier

3 sprays each comprising 1 orange arum lily, yellow roses and buds, purple sweet peas, autumnal beech leaves and rose leaves

Cake

Top Tier: 20cm (8") Petal

Middle Tier: 25cm (10") Petal

Bottom Tier: 30cm (12") Petal

Boards

Top Tier: 25cm (10") Petal drum

Middle Tier: 25cm (10") Petal (hidden)

Bottom Tier: 40cm (16") Petal drum

Marzipan

Top Tier: 570g (1$^{1}/_{4}$lb)

Middle Tier: 910g (2lb)

Bottom Tier: 1.14kg (2$^{1}/_{2}$lb)

Sugarpaste

Demerara

Top Tier: 570g (1$^{1}/_{4}$lb)

Middle Tier: 910g (2lb)

Bottom Tier: 1.14kg (2$^{1}/_{2}$lb)

Royal Icing

Demerara

Ribbons

15mm moss green ribbon

2mm braid (purple/orange/yellow)

Pillars/Separators

3 x 11cm (4$^{1}/_{4}$") SK Barley Twist pillars (dusted light gold)

Colours

SK Metallic Lustre Dust: Light Gold

Piping Nozzles

No. 1

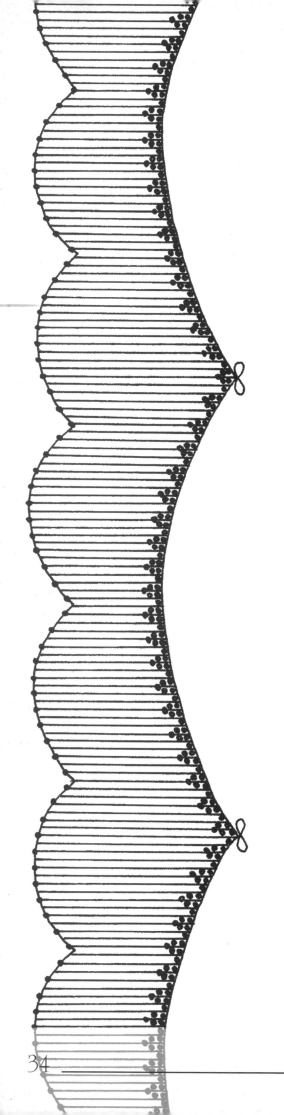

ISABELLE

REQUIREMENTS

Flowers/Leaves

All Tiers

Ivory open roses and buds set against clusters of pale blue/lilac hydrangea flowers, sprays of purple and mauve sweet peas, and large rose leaves

Cake

Top Tier: 15cm (6") Round

Upper Middle Tier: 20cm (8") Round

Lower Middle Tier: 25cm (10") Round

Bottom Tier: 30cm (12") Round

Boards

Top Tier: 20cm (8") Round drum

Upper Middle Tier: 25cm (10") Round drum

Lower Middle Tier: 30cm (12") Round drum

Bottom Tier: 40cm (16") Round drum

Marzipan

Top Tier: 340g ($^3/_4$lb)

Upper Middle Tier: 570g ($1^1/_4$lb)

Lower Middle Tier: 950g (2lb 1oz)

Bottom Tier: 1.14kg ($2^1/_2$lb)

Sugarpaste

Colour: Ivory

Top Tier: 340g ($^3/_4$lb)

Upper Middle Tier: 570g ($1^1/_4$lb)

Lower Middle Tier: 950g (2lb 1oz)

Bottom Tier: 1.14kg ($2^1/_2$lb)

Royal Icing

Ivory coloured

Ribbons

15mm iris ribbon and 32 x 1.5mm iris bows

Pillars/Separators

Oasis blocks, well covered in cling film

Plastic dowels

Colours

SK Paste Food Colour: Berberis (use a hint to give ivory)

Piping Nozzles

Nos. 0 and 1

Refer to page 34 (Isabelle) for template

COURTNEY

REQUIREMENTS

Flowers/Leaves

Top Tier

7 ivory arum lilies set against Freesias, Hypericum berries, ivory roses and buds, rose leaves, and variegated ivy leaves

Middle and Bottom Tiers

Sprays of variegated ivy leaves

Cake

Top Tier: 20cm (8") Round

Middle Tier: 25cm (10") Round

Bottom Tier: 30cm (12") Round

Boards

Top Tier: 25cm (10") Round drum

Middle Tier: 30cm (12") Round drum

Bottom Tier: 40cm (16") Round drum

Marzipan

Top Tier: 570g (1^1/$_4$lb)

Middle Tier: 950g (2lb 1oz)

Bottom Tier: 1.14kg (2^1/$_2$lb)

Sugarpaste

Colour: Ivory

Top Tier: 570g (1^1/$_4$lb)

Middle Tier: 950g (2lb 1oz)

Bottom Tier: 1.14kg (2^1/$_2$lb)

Royal Icing

Ivory coloured

Ribbons

15mm ivory ribbon and 2mm gold/cream twisted braid

Pillars/Separators

3 x cake drums:

10cm (4"), 15cm (6") and 20cm (8")

Colours

SK Paste Food Colour: Berberis (use a hint to give ivory)

Piping Nozzles

Nos. 0 and 1

 LLA

REQUIREMENTS

Flowers/Leaves

All Tiers

1 spray on each tier comprising 5 full Christmas roses, 3 half-open Christmas roses and 3 buds set against holly berry and gold berry clusters, dark green holly leaf sprays, and variegated ivy leaves

Cake

Top Tier: 15cm (6") Round

Middle Tier: 20cm (8") Round

Bottom Tier: 25cm (10") Round

Boards

Top Tier: 20cm (8") Round drum

Middle Tier: 25cm (10") Round drum

Bottom Tier: 36cm (14") Round drum

Marzipan

Top Tier: 340g ($^3/_4$lb)

Middle Tier: 570g ($1^1/_4$lb)

Bottom Tier: 950g (2lb 1oz)

Sugarpaste

Colour: White

Top Tier: 340g ($^3/_4$lb)

Middle Tier: 570g ($1^1/_4$lb)

Bottom Tier: 950g (2lb 1oz)

Royal Icing

White

Ribbons

15mm red

Pillars/Separators

6 x 7.5cm (3") round tear drop pillars

Colours

SK Metallic Lustre Dust: Light Gold

Piping Nozzles

No. 1

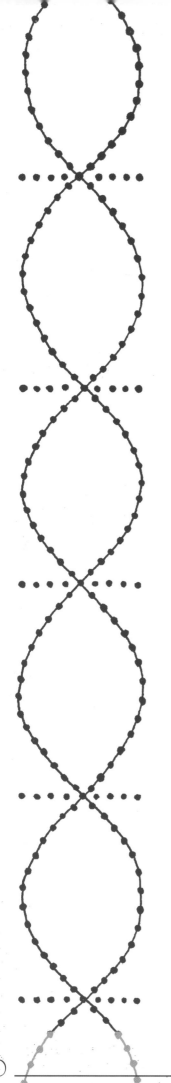

PHILIPPA

REQUIREMENTS

Flowers/Leaves

Middle Tier

7 Alstroemeria lilies set against pale pink rose buds, Singapore orchids, sprays of Star of Bethlehem, and rose leaves

Bottom Tier

1 Alstroemeria lily with 1 rose leaf

Cake

Top Tier: 13cm (5") Round

Middle Tier: 25cm (10") Round

Bottom Tier: 36cm (14") Round

Boards

Top Tier: 15cm (6") Round

Middle Tier: 25cm (10") Round (hidden)

Bottom Tier: 50cm (20") Round drum

Marzipan

Top Tier: 260g (9oz)

Middle Tier: 950g (2lb 1oz)

Bottom Tier: 1.36kg (3lb)

Sugarpaste

Colour: White

Top Tier: 260g (9oz)

Middle Tier: 950g (2lb 1oz)

Bottom Tier: 1.36kg (3lb)

Decoration

Bride and groom figurine

Royal Icing

White

Ribbons

3mm and 15mm blue

Pillars/Separators

Candlestick

Colours

SK Dust Food Colour: Cyclamen (to give burgundy)

Piping Nozzles

Nos. 0 and 1

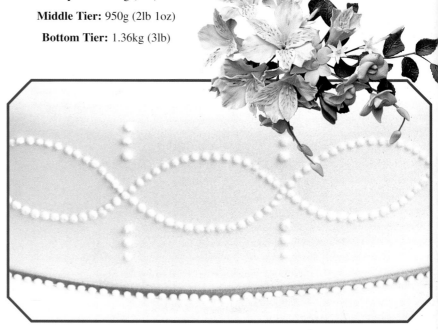

FLOELLA

REQUIREMENTS

Cake

Top Tier: 15cm (6") Round

Middle Tier: 25cm (10") Round

Bottom Tier: 36cm (14") Round

Boards

Top Tier: 15cm (6") Round (hidden)

Middle Tier: 25cm (10") Round (hidden)

Bottom Tier: 46cm (18") Round drum

Marzipan

Top Tier: 340g (³/₄lb)

Middle Tier: 950g (2lb 1oz)

Bottom Tier: 1.36kg (3lb)

Sugarpaste

Colour: White

Top Tier: 340g (³/₄lb)

Middle Tier: 950g (2lb 1oz)

Bottom Tier: 1.36kg (3lb)

Decoration

Top Tier

1 crown (made using a church door cutter, and heart and honeysuckle cutters), feathers and dropped pearl beads

All Tiers

Sugarpaste butterflies

Royal Icing

White

Ribbons

15mm pale blue, 3mm light blue, lilac and blue (plaited)

Colours

SK Lustre Dusts: various shades

Piping Nozzles

No. 1

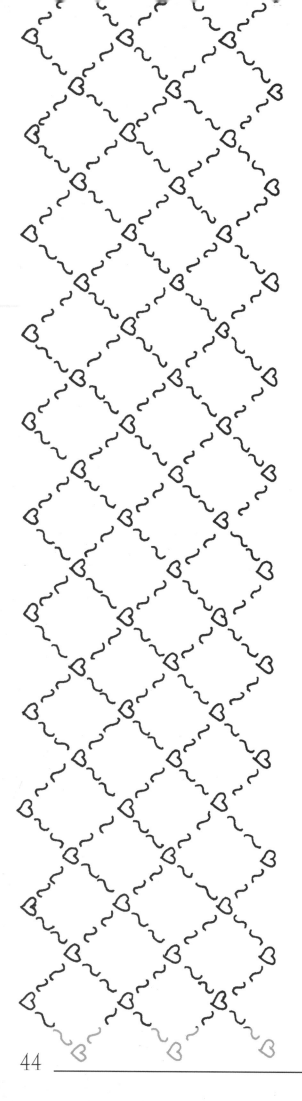

QUEENIE

REQUIREMENTS

Flowers/Leaves

Top Tier

3 half-open arum lilies set against sprays of yellow roses and buds, jasmine, rose leaves, variegated leaves, and sprigs of gold Gypsophila

Middle Tier

3 sprays each comprising 1 open arum lily, 1 yellow rose, rose buds and leaves, jasmine, variegated leaves and sprigs of gold Gypsophila

Bottom Tier

3 sprays each comprising 2 open arum lilies, 1 yellow rose, rose buds and leaves, jasmine, variegated leaves and sprigs of gold Gypsophila

Cake

Top Tier: 10cm (4") Hexagonal
15cm (6") Hexagonal

Middle Tier: 20cm (8") Hexagonal
25cm (10") Hexagonal

Bottom Tier: 30cm (12") Hexagonal
35cm (14") Hexagonal

Boards

Top Tier: 10cm (4") Hexagonal (hidden)
20cm (8") Hexagonal drum

Middle Tier: 20cm (8") Hexagonal (hidden)
30cm (12") Hexagonal drum

Bottom Tier: 30cm (12") Hexagonal (hidden)
40cm (16") Hexagonal drum

Marzipan

Top Tier: 910g (2lb)
Middle Tier: 1.8kg (4lb)
Bottom Tier: 3.4kg (7$^1/_2$lb)

Sugarpaste

Colour: White
Top Tier: 910g (2lb)

Middle Tier: 1.8kg (4lb)
Bottom Tier: 3.4kg (7$^1/_2$lb)

Royal Icing

White

Ribbons

15mm white ribbon, thin gold thread, thin silver thread

Pillars/Separators

6 x 14cm (5$^1/_2$") SK Barley Twist Pillars: White

Colours

SK Metallic Lustre Dusts: Light Gold, Light Silver

Special Tools

Kemper tool: heart plunger cutter (you will need approx 1700 hearts)

Piping Nozzles

No.1

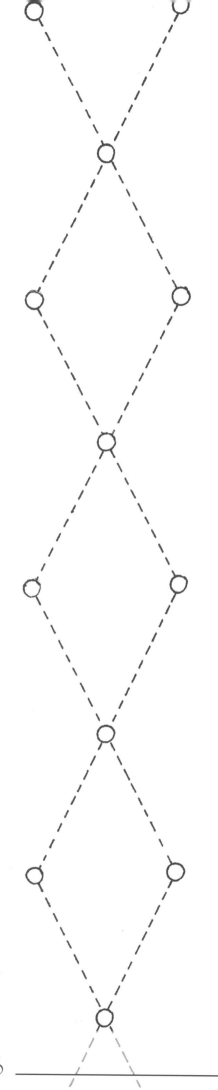

BELINDA

Requirements

Flowers/Leaves

Top Tier

4 medium ruby roses set against ruby rose buds, sprays of rose leaves and sprigs of Gypsophila

Cake

Top Tier: 15cm (6") Round

Middle Tier: 20cm (8") Round

Bottom Tier: 25cm (10") Round

Boards

Top Tier: 15cm (6") Round (hidden)

Middle Tier: 20cm (8") Round (hidden)

Bottom Tier: 36cm (14") Round drum

Marzipan

Top Tier: 340g ($^3/_4$lb)

Middle Tier: 570g ($1^1/_4$lb)

Bottom Tier: 950g (2lb 1oz)

Sugarpaste

Colour: White

Top Tier: 340g ($^3/_4$lb)

Middle Tier: 570g ($1^1/_4$lb)

Bottom Tier: 950g (2lb 1oz)

Royal Icing

White

Ribbons

15mm wine

Colours

SK Paste Food Colour: Leaf Green, Ruby

Piping Nozzles

No. 2

Special Tools

Rose bud embosser (or use a freehand method)

Natasha

Requirements

Flowers/Leaves

Top Tier

4 white orchids set against blossom sprays and ivy leaves

Middle Tier

2 sprays each comprising 2 white orchids set against blossom sprays and ivy leaves

Bottom Tier

2 sprays each comprising 3 white orchids set against blossom sprays and ivy leaves

Cake

Top Tier: 20cm (8") Diamond
Middle Tier: 25cm (10") Diamond
Bottom Tier: 30cm (12") Diamond

Boards

Top Tier: 25cm (10") Diamond drum
Middle Tier: 30cm (12") Diamond drum
Bottom Tier: 40cm (16") Diamond drum

Marzipan

Top Tier: 800g ($1^3/_4$lb)
Middle Tier: 1.02kg ($2^1/_4$lb)
Bottom Tier: 1.25kg ($2^3/_4$lb)

Sugarpaste

Colour: Bluebell (use demerara sugarpaste)
Top Tier: 800g ($1^3/_4$lb)
Middle Tier: 1.02kg ($2^1/_4$lb)

Bottom Tier: 1.25kg ($2^3/_4$lb)

Decoration

5mm silver dragees (used in side design)

Royal Icing

White

Ribbons

15mm ivory

Pillars/Separators

8 x SK Ivy Pillars (dusted light gold)

Colours

SK Paste Food Colour: Bluebell

SK Metallic Lustre Dust: Light Gold

Piping Nozzles

No. 1

TOP TIER

BOTTOM TIER

MIDDLE TIER

INGRID

REQUIREMENTS

Flowers/Leaves

Vase Arrangement

30 open and half-open primroses set against primrose buds and leaves

Top Tier

4 side sprays each comprising 6 assorted primroses, 1 bud and 3 leaves

Middle Tier

4 side sprays each comprising 7 assorted primroses, 1 bud and 3 leaves

Bottom Tier

4 side sprays each comprising 7 assorted primroses, 1 bud and 3 leaves

Cake

Top Tier: 20cm (8") Square

Middle Tier: 25cm (10") Square

Bottom Tier: 30cm (12") Square

Boards

Top Tier: 25cm (10") Square drum

Middle Tier: 30cm (12") Square drum

Bottom Tier: 36cm (14") Square drum

Marzipan

Top Tier: 800g ($1^3/_4$lb)

Middle Tier: 1.02kg ($2^1/_4$lb)

Bottom Tier: 1.25kg ($2^3/_4$lb)

Sugarpaste

Colour: White

Top Tier: 800g ($1^3/_4$lb)

Middle Tier: 1.02kg ($2^1/_4$lb)

Bottom Tier: 1.25kg ($2^3/_4$lb)

Royal Icing

White

Ribbons

15mm white

Pillars/Separators

Cake drums (to be used as separators)

Colours

SK Metallic Lustre Dust: Light Gold

Piping Nozzles

Nos. 0 and 1

Special Tools

Elegant Creations: diamond cross cutter

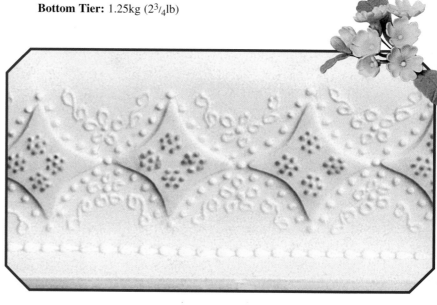

ROSALIE

REQUIREMENTS

Flowers/Leaves

All Tiers

Small sprays comprising pink rose buds and rose leaves

Cake

Top Tier: 15cm (6") Round

Bottom Tier: 30cm (12") Round

Boards

Top Tier: 25cm (10") Round drum

Bottom Tier: 36cm (14") Round drum

Base Board: 40cm (16") Round drum

Marzipan

Top Tier: 340g ($^3/_4$lb)

Bottom Tier: 1.14kg ($2^1/_2$lb)

Sugarpaste

Colour: White

Top Tier: 340g ($^3/_4$lb)

Bottom Tier: 1.14kg ($2^1/_2$lb)

Royal Icing

White

Ribbons

15mm pale pink

Pillars/Separators

Wilton 'Always and Forever' separator ring

Piping Nozzles

No. 42

Special Tools

Corteil & Barratt Mould: Double Sided
Blossom Lace (SL029)

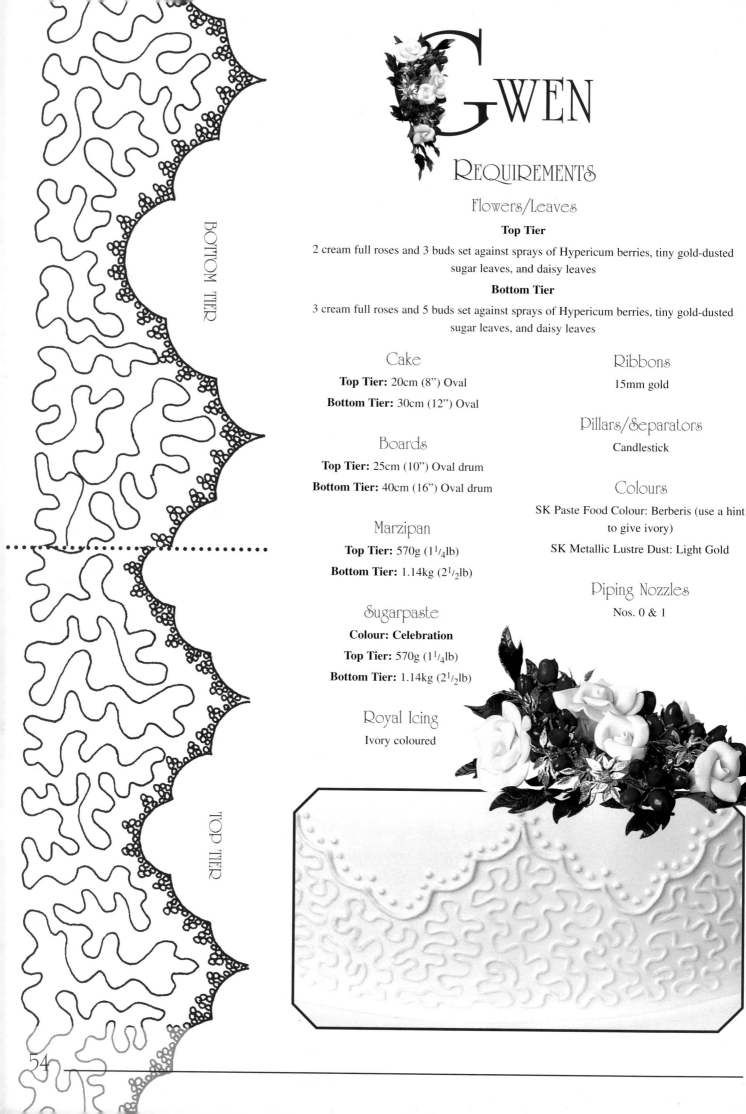

BOTTOM TIER

TOP TIER

GWEN

REQUIREMENTS

Flowers/Leaves

Top Tier

2 cream full roses and 3 buds set against sprays of Hypericum berries, tiny gold-dusted sugar leaves, and daisy leaves

Bottom Tier

3 cream full roses and 5 buds set against sprays of Hypericum berries, tiny gold-dusted sugar leaves, and daisy leaves

Cake

Top Tier: 20cm (8") Oval

Bottom Tier: 30cm (12") Oval

Boards

Top Tier: 25cm (10") Oval drum

Bottom Tier: 40cm (16") Oval drum

Marzipan

Top Tier: 570g (1¼lb)

Bottom Tier: 1.14kg (2½lb)

Sugarpaste

Colour: Celebration

Top Tier: 570g (1¼lb)

Bottom Tier: 1.14kg (2½lb)

Royal Icing

Ivory coloured

Ribbons

15mm gold

Pillars/Separators

Candlestick

Colours

SK Paste Food Colour: Berberis (use a hint to give ivory)

SK Metallic Lustre Dust: Light Gold

Piping Nozzles

Nos. 0 & 1

CLARISSA

REQUIREMENTS

Flowers/Leaves

Top Tier
4 white orchids with 4 orchid leaves
Bottom Tier
6 white orchids with 4 orchid leaves

Cake

Top Tier: 20cm (8") Heart
Bottom Tier: 30cm (12") Heart

Boards

Top Tier: 25cm (10") Heart drum
Bottom Tier: 40cm (16") Heart drum

Marzipan

Top Tier: 570g (1^1/$_4$lb)
Bottom Tier: 1.14kg (2^1/$_2$lb)

Sugarpaste

Colour: White
Top Tier: 570g (1^1/$_4$lb)
Bottom Tier: 1.14kg (2^1/$_2$lb)

Royal Icing

Demerara

Ribbons

15mm green

Pillars/Separators

2-tier chrome step stand

Colours

SK Paste Food Colour: Rose

(painted onto side design)

Piping Nozzles

No. 1

MARIE

REQUIREMENTS

Flowers/Leaves

Top Tier

4 purple arum lilies set against sprays of pink roses, lilac Freesias and sprays of ivy leaves

Bottom Tier

5 purple arum lilies set against sprays of pink roses, lilac Freesias and sprays of ivy leaves

Cake

Top Tier: 20cm (8") Oval

Bottom Tier: 36cm (14") Oval

Boards

Top Tier: 25cm (10") Oval drum

Bottom Tier: 40cm (16") Oval drum

Marzipan

Top Tier: 570g (1$\frac{1}{4}$lb)

Bottom Tier: 1.36kg (3lb)

Sugarpaste

Colour: Pale Pink

Top Tier: 570g (1$\frac{1}{4}$lb)

Bottom Tier: 1.36kg (3lb)

Royal Icing

Demerara

Ribbons

15mm purple

Pillars/Separators

Candlestick

Colours

SK Paste Food Colour: Rose

SK Bridal Satin Lustre Dust: Alabaster

Piping Nozzles

Nos. 0 and 1

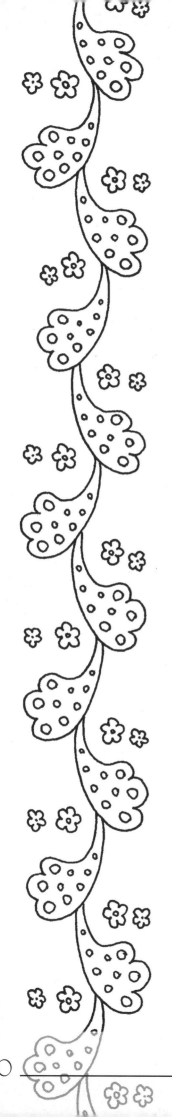

ROWENA

REQUIREMENTS

Flowers/Leaves

Top Tier

2 open ivory roses and 3 buds set against sprays of Star of Bethlehem, rosehip, autumnal oak and beech leaves, and plain leaves

Bottom Tier

4 open ivory roses, 3 half-open ivory roses and 3 buds set against sprays of Star of Bethlehem, rosehip, autumnal oak and beech leaves, and plain leaves

Cake

Top Tier: 20cm (8") Oval

Bottom Tier: 30cm (12") Oval

Boards

Top Tier: 25cm (10") Oval drum

Bottom Tier: 40cm (16") Oval drum

Marzipan

Top Tier: 570g (1^1/$_4$lb)

Bottom Tier: 1.14kg (2^1/$_2$lb)

Sugarpaste

Demerara

Top Tier: 570g (1^1/$_4$lb)

Bottom Tier: 1.14kg (2^1/$_2$lb)

Royal Icing

Demerara and ivory coloured

Ribbons

15mm gold

Pillars/Separators

2-tier chrome "C" stand

Colours

SK Paste Food Colour: Berberis (use a hint to give ivory)

Piping Nozzles

No. 1

Special Tools

PME small and medium blossom plunger cutters (for side design)

PAIGE

REQUIREMENTS

Flowers/Leaves

Top Tier

3 medium ruby roses and 15 buds set against small sprays of ivy leaves

Middle Tier

4 sprays each comprising 2 medium ruby roses, 1 rose bud, single rose leaves and single ivy leaves

Bottom Tier

4 sprays each comprising 3 medium ruby roses, 3 rose buds, sprays of rose leaves and sprays of ivy leaves

Cake

Top Tier: 20cm (8") Scalloped oval

Middle Tier: 25cm (10") Scalloped oval

Bottom Tier: 30cm (12") Scalloped oval

Boards

Top Tier: 25cm (10") Scalloped oval drum

Middle Tier: 30cm (12") Scalloped oval drum

Bottom Tier: 40cm (16") Scalloped oval drum

Marzipan

Top Tier: 570g (1^1/$_4$lb)

Middle Tier: 950g (2lb 1oz)

Bottom Tier: 1.14kg (2^1/$_2$lb)

Sugarpaste

Colour: Celebration

Top Tier: 570g (1^1/$_4$lb)

Middle Tier: 950g (2lb 1oz)

Bottom Tier: 1.14kg (2^1/$_2$lb)

Royal Icing

Ivory coloured

Ribbons

15mm ivory

Pillars/Separators

8 x 7.5cm (3") round pillars

Colours

SK Dust Food Colour: Cyclamen (to give burgundy)

Piping Nozzles

No.1

FERN

REQUIREMENTS

Flowers/Leaves

Top Tier

Yellow, ivory and lemon Narcissus sprays set against sprays of montbretia, primroses, mauve Freesias, primrose leaves, and sprays of plain leaves

Bottom Tier

Yellow, ivory and lemon Narcissus sprays set against sprays of montbretia, primroses, mauve Freesias, primrose leaves, and sprays of plain leaves

Cake

Top Tier: 20cm (8") Scalloped oval

Bottom Tier: 30cm (12") Scalloped oval

Boards

Top Tier: 25cm (10") Scalloped oval

Bottom Tier: 40cm (16") Scalloped oval

Marzipan

Top Tier: 570g (1$\frac{1}{4}$lb)

Bottom Tier: 1.14kg (2$\frac{1}{2}$lb)

Sugarpaste

Colour: Fawn

Top Tier: 570g (1$\frac{1}{4}$lb)

Bottom Tier: 1.14kg (2$\frac{1}{2}$lb)

Royal Icing

Ivory coloured

Ribbons

3mm and 15mm iris

Pillars/Separators

4 x 7.5cm (3") round pillars

Colours

SK Paste Food Colour: Bulrush (use a hint to give fawn)

Piping Nozzles

Nos. 0 and 1

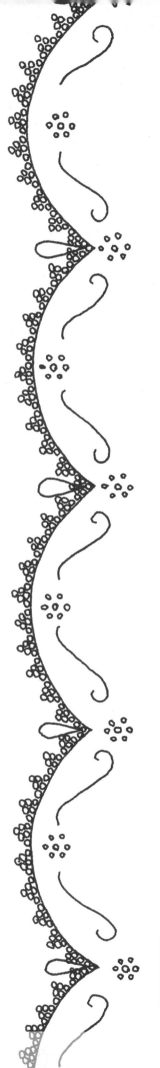

Tabitha

Requirements

Flowers/Leaves

Top Tier

4 deep orange lilies set against peach sweet peas, sprays of Hypericum berries, daisy leaves and plain leaves

Bottom Tier

6 deep orange lilies set against peach sweet peas, sprays of Hypericum berries, daisy leaves and plain leaves

Cake

Top Tier: 20cm (8") Heart

Bottom Tier: 30cm (12") Heart

Boards

Top Tier: 25cm (10") Heart drum

Bottom Tier: 40cm (16") Heart drum

Marzipan

Top Tier: 570g ($1^1/_4$lb)

Bottom Tier: 1.14kg ($2^1/_2$lb)

Sugarpaste

Colour: Pale peach

Top Tier: 570g ($1^1/_4$lb)

Bottom Tier: 1.14kg ($2^1/_2$lb)

Decoration

Sugar butterflies

1 small (top tier) and 1 large (bottom tier)

Royal Icing

Ivory coloured

Ribbons

15mm peach and 5mm blue

Pillars/Separators

2-tier chrome "C" stand

Colours

SK Paste Food Colour: Berberis (use hint to give ivory), Nasturtium (use a hint to give peach)

Piping Nozzles

Nos. 0 and 1

Special Tools

Hawthorne Hill Butterfly Moulds: Small tortoiseshell, Exotic No. 7

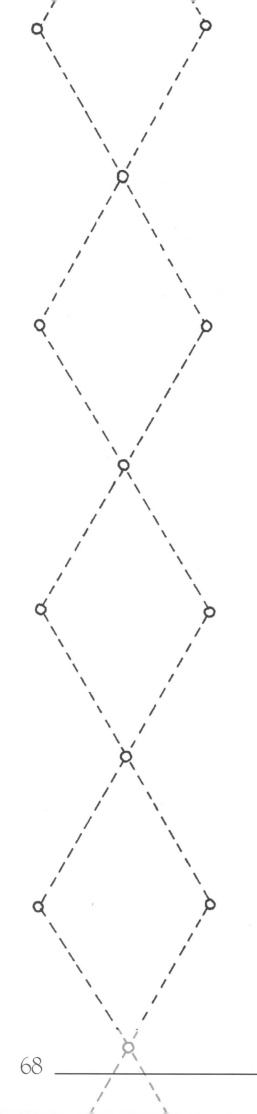

GABRIELLA

REQUIREMENTS

Flowers/Leaves

Top Tier

2 open Stargazer lilies and 1 bud set against sprays of rose buds, purple sweet peas, pale pink Star of Bethlehem, eucalyptus leaves, ivy leaves, and rose leaves

Bottom Tier

4 open Stargazer lilies and 1 bud set against sprays of rose buds, purple sweet peas, pale pink Star of Bethlehem, eucalyptus leaves, ivy leaves, and rose leaves

Cake

Top Tier: 20cm (8") Oval

Bottom Tier: 30cm (12") Oval

Boards

Top Tier: 25cm (10") Oval drum

Bottom Tier: 40cm (16") Oval drum

Marzipan

Top Tier: 570g (1¹/₄lb)

Bottom Tier: 1.14kg (2¹/₂lb)

Sugarpaste

Colour: Violet (use demerara sugarpaste)

Top Tier: 570g (1¹/₄lb)

Bottom Tier: 1.14kg (2¹/₂lb)

Royal Icing

Ivory coloured

Ribbons

15mm gold

Pillars/Separators

2-tier chrome "C" stand

Colours

SK Paste Food Colour: Violet

Piping Nozzles

No. 1

Special Tools

Elegant Creations: Fleur de Lys cutter

(use Demerara sugarpaste)

WHITNEY

REQUIREMENTS

Flowers/Leaves

Top Tier

1 Casablanca lily set against ruby roses and buds, sprays of Star of Bethlehem, pearl clusters, fern leaves and sprays of eucalyptus leaves

Bottom Tier

1 Casablanca lily set against ruby roses and buds, sprays of Star of Bethlehem, pearl clusters, fern leaves, sprays of eucalyptus leaves, and plain ivory leaves dusted with SK Myrtle

Cake

Top Tier: 15cm (6") Round

Bottom Tier: 30cm (12") Round

Boards

Top Tier: 20cm (8") Round drum

Bottom Tier: 38cm (15") Round drum

Base: 50cm (20") round drum (covered with snow leopard patterned fabric)

Marzipan

Top Tier: 340g ($^3/_4$lb)

Bottom Tier: 1.14kg ($2^1/_2$lb)

Sugarpaste

Colour: White

Top Tier: 340g ($^3/_4$lb)

Bottom Tier: 1.14kg ($2^1/_2$lb)

Royal Icing

White

Ribbons

15mm black plaited braid

Pillars/Separators

1 x separator (covered with snow leopard patterned fabric)

Colours

SK Bridal Satin Lustre Dust: Myrtle

Piping Nozzles

No. 1.5

VALENTINE

REQUIREMENTS

Flowers/Leaves

All Tiers

1 spray on each tier comprising 2 medium and 2 large red roses, 1 red rose bud, and sprays of rose leaves

Cake

Top Tier: 15cm (6") Hexagonal

Middle Tier: 20cm (8") Hexagonal

Bottom Tier: 25cm (10") Hexagonal

Boards

Top Tier: 20cm (8") Hexagonal drum

Middle Tier: 25cm (10") Hexagonal drum

Bottom Tier: 36cm (14") Hexagonal drum

Marzipan

Top Tier: 500g (1lb 1oz)

Middle Tier: 800g (1³/₄lb)

Bottom Tier: 1.02kg (2¹/₄lb)

Sugarpaste

Colour: White

Top Tier: 500g (1lb 1oz)

Middle Tier: 800g (1³/₄lb)

Bottom Tier: 1.02kg (2¹/₄lb)

Royal Icing

White

Ribbons

15mm red

Pillars/Separators

6 x hexagonal teardrop pillars

Colours

SK Metallic Lustre Dust: Light Gold

Piping Nozzles

Nos. 1 and 2

Special Tools

FMM heart cutters (in 3 sizes; for use as embossers)

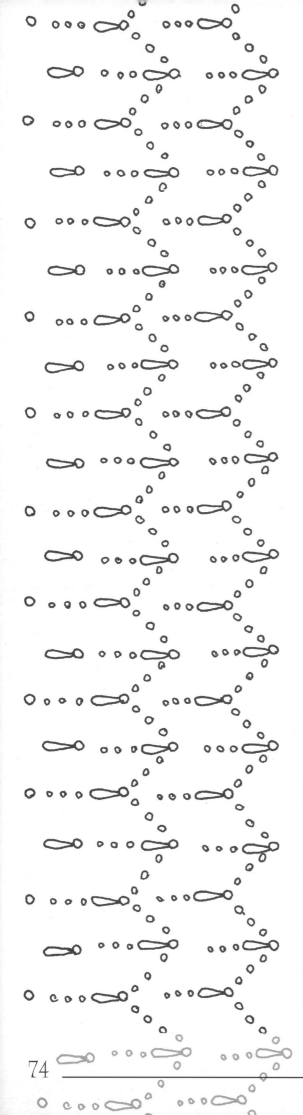

TIFFANY

REQUIREMENTS

Flowers/Leaves

Top Tier

4 red lily sprays set against sprays of blossoms and fern leaves (silk)

Bottom Tier

9 red lily sprays set against sprays of blossoms and fern leaves (silk)

Cake

Top Tier: 15cm (6") Round

Bottom Tier: 25cm (10") Round

Boards

Top Tier: 20cm (8") Round drum

Bottom Tier: 30cm (12") Round drum

Marzipan

Top Tier: 340g ($^3/_4$lb)

Bottom Tier: 950g (2lb 1oz)

Sugarpaste

Colour: White

Top Tier: 340g ($^3/_4$lb)

Bottom Tier: 950g (2lb 1oz)

Royal Icing

White

Ribbons

15mm gold

Pillars/Separators

2-tier chrome "C" stand

Colours

SK Metallic Lustre Dust: Light Gold

Piping Nozzles

No. 1

BRITTANY

REQUIREMENTS

Flowers/Leaves

Top Tier

13 ruby rose buds set against sprays of blossoms and ivy leaves

Upper Middle Tier

3 sprays each comprising 2 ruby roses and 1 bud, sprays of blossoms and ivy leaves

Middle Tier

3 sprays each comprising 2 ruby roses and 1 bud, sprays of blossoms and ivy leaves

Lower Middle Tier

3 sprays each comprising 2 ruby roses and 3 buds, sprays of blossoms and ivy leaves

Bottom Tier

3 sprays each comprising 2 ruby roses and 3 buds, sprays of blossoms and ivy leaves

Cake

Top Tier: 15cm (6") Hexagonal

Upper Middle Tier: 20cm (8") Hexagonal

Middle Tier: 25cm (10") Hexagonal

Lower Middle Tier: 30cm (12") Hexagonal

Bottom Tier: 35cm (14") Hexagonal

Boards

Top Tier: 20cm (8") Hexagonal drum

Upper Middle Tier: 25cm (10") Hexagonal drum

Middle Tier: 30cm (12") Hexagonal drum

Lower Middle Tier: 35cm (14") Hexagonal drum

Bottom Tier: 40cm (16") Hexagonal

Marzipan

Top Tier: 500g (1lb 1oz)

Upper Middle Tier: 800g (1^3/$_4$lb)

Middle Tier: 1.02kg (2^1/$_4$lb)

Lower Middle Tier: 1.14kg (2^1/$_2$lb)

Bottom Tier: 1.36kg (3lb)

Sugarpaste

Demerara

Top Tier: 500g (1lb 1oz)

Upper Middle Tier: 800g (1^3/$_4$lb)

Middle Tier: 1.02kg (2^1/$_4$lb)

Lower Middle Tier: 1.14kg (2^1/$_2$lb)

Bottom Tier: 1.36kg (3lb)

Royal Icing

Ivory coloured

Ribbons

15mm sand colour

Pillars/Separators

12 x 7.5cm (3") hexagonal pillars

Colours

SK Paste Food Colour: Berberis (use a hint to give ivory)

Piping Nozzles

No. 0

Special Tools

Kemper tool: heart plunger cutter (you will need approximately 1000 hearts)

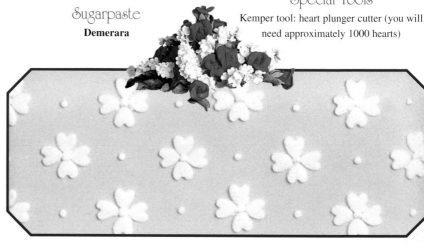

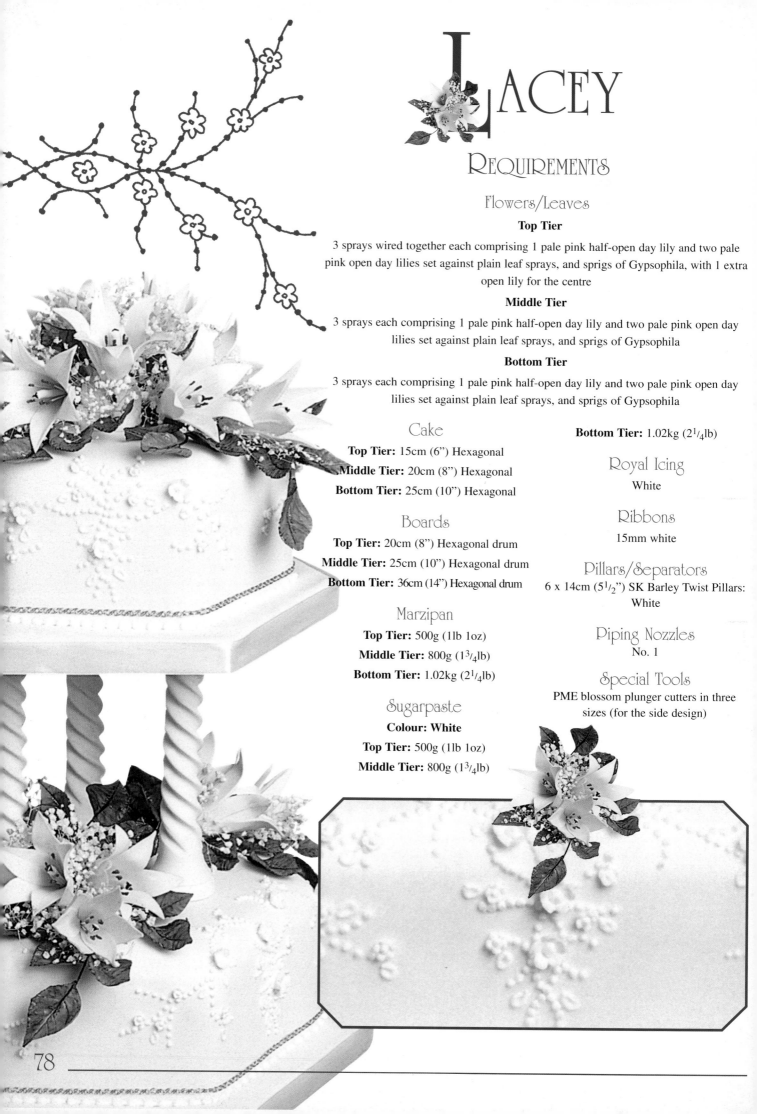

Lacey

Requirements

Flowers/Leaves

Top Tier

3 sprays wired together each comprising 1 pale pink half-open day lily and two pale pink open day lilies set against plain leaf sprays, and sprigs of Gypsophila, with 1 extra open lily for the centre

Middle Tier

3 sprays each comprising 1 pale pink half-open day lily and two pale pink open day lilies set against plain leaf sprays, and sprigs of Gypsophila

Bottom Tier

3 sprays each comprising 1 pale pink half-open day lily and two pale pink open day lilies set against plain leaf sprays, and sprigs of Gypsophila

Cake

Top Tier: 15cm (6") Hexagonal
Middle Tier: 20cm (8") Hexagonal
Bottom Tier: 25cm (10") Hexagonal

Boards

Top Tier: 20cm (8") Hexagonal drum
Middle Tier: 25cm (10") Hexagonal drum
Bottom Tier: 36cm (14") Hexagonal drum

Marzipan

Top Tier: 500g (1lb 1oz)
Middle Tier: 800g ($1^3/_4$lb)
Bottom Tier: 1.02kg ($2^1/_4$lb)

Sugarpaste

Colour: White
Top Tier: 500g (1lb 1oz)
Middle Tier: 800g ($1^3/_4$lb)

Bottom Tier: 1.02kg ($2^1/_4$lb)

Royal Icing

White

Ribbons

15mm white

Pillars/Separators

6 x 14cm ($5^1/_2$") SK Barley Twist Pillars: White

Piping Nozzles

No. 1

Special Tools

PME blossom plunger cutters in three sizes (for the side design)

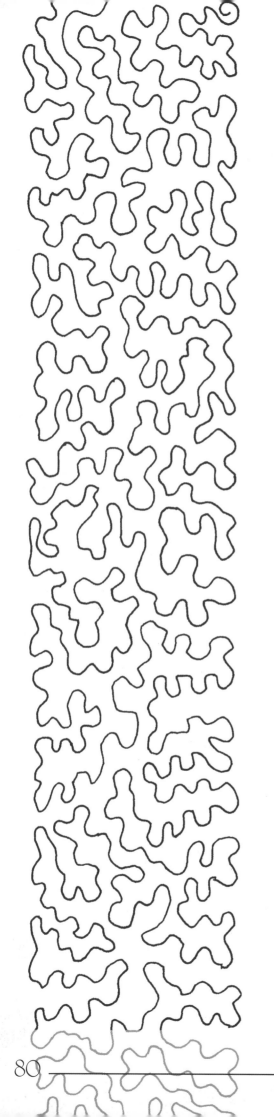

GEENA

REQUIREMENTS

Flowers/Leaves

Top Tier

3 large Cattleya orchids set against sprays of blossoms, orchid leaves, and bunches of plastic grapes

Bottom Tier

6 large Cattleya orchids set against sprays of blossoms, plain leaves, orchid leaves, and bunches of plastic grapes

Cake

Top Tier: 20cm (8") Petal

Bottom Tier: 30cm (12") Petal

Boards

Top Tier: 25cm (10") Petal drum

Bottom Tier: 40cm (16") Petal drum

Marzipan

Top Tier: 680g (1^1/$_2$lb)

Bottom Tier: 1.25kg (2^3/$_4$lb)

Sugarpaste

Colour: White

Top Tier: 680g (1^1/$_2$lb)

Bottom Tier: 1.25kg (2^3/$_4$lb)

Royal Icing

Terracotta coloured

Ribbons

15mm terracotta

Pillars/Separators

SK Cupid Pillar (with board and dowels for support)

Colours

SK Paste Food Colour: Terracotta

Piping Nozzles

No.1

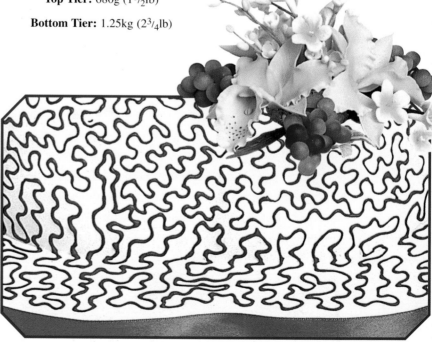

See page 127 for the top design template

MOLLY

REQUIREMENTS

Flowers/Leaves

Top Tier

1 Casablanca lily set against sprays of Star of Bethlehem, ruby roses and buds, fern leaves, sprays of plain ivory leaves, eucalyptus leaves, and pearl clusters

Bottom Tier

1 Casablanca lily set against sprays of Star of Bethlehem, ruby roses and buds, fern leaves, sprays of plain ivory leaves, eucalyptus leaves, and pearl clusters

Cake

Top Tier: 20cm (8") Petal

Bottom Tier: 30cm (12") Petal

Boards

Top Tier: 25cm (10") Petal drum

Bottom Tier: 40cm (16") Petal drum

Marzipan

Top Tier: 680g (1$^{1}/_{2}$lb)

Bottom Tier: 1.25kg (2$^{3}/_{4}$lb)

Sugarpaste

Colour: Pale Blue

Top Tier: 680g (1$^{1}/_{2}$lb)

Bottom Tier: 1.25kg (2$^{3}/_{4}$lb)

Royal Icing

White

Ribbons

15mm aqua blue/green

10mm pearled braid

Pillars/Separators

1 x 30cm (12") SK Corinthian Pillar

Colours

SK Paste Food Colour: Baby Blue

Piping Nozzles

Nos. 0 and 1

PANDORA

REQUIREMENTS

Flowers/Leaves

All Tiers

4 dark blue Anemones

Cake

Top Tier: 15cm (6") Round

Middle Tier: (8") Square

Bottom Tier: 30cm (12") Round

Boards

Top Tier: 15cm (6") Round (hidden)

Middle Tier: (8") Square (hidden)

Bottom Tier: 40cm (16") Square drum

Marzipan

Top Tier: 340g (^{3}/$_4$lb)

Middle Tier: 800g (1^3/$_4$lb)

Bottom Tier: 1.14kg (2^1/$_2$lb)

Sugarpaste

Colour: Demerara and ivory coloured

Top Tier: 340g (^{3}/$_4$lb) (demerara)

Middle Tier: 800g (1^3/$_4$lb) (ivory)

Bottom Tier: 1.14kg (2^1/$_2$lb) (demerara)

Royal Icing

Demerara

Ribbons

5cm (2") twisted blue and 15mm blue

Colours

SK Metallic Lustre Dust: Light Gold

SK Paste Food Colour: Berberis (use a hint to give ivory)

Piping Nozzles

No. 1

Special Tools

Pinking scissors

Elegant Creations: Fleur de Lys cutter

Hazel

Requirements

Flowers/Leaves

Top Tier

4 open ivory day lilies set against sprays of oak leaves, rosehip, ears of wheat, and autumnal oak leaves (for the side design)

Middle Tier

2 open ivory day lilies set against sprays of oak leaves, rosehip, ears of wheat, and autumnal oak leaves (for the side design)

Cake

Top Tier: 20cm (8") Scalloped oval

Middle Tier: 25cm (10") Scalloped oval

Bottom Tier: 30cm (12") Scalloped oval

Boards

Top Tier: 25cm (10") Scalloped oval drum

Middle Tier: 30cm (12") Scalloped oval (hidden)

Bottom Tier: 40cm (16") Scalloped oval drum

Marzipan

Top Tier: 570g (1^1/$_4$lb)

Middle Tier: 950g (2lb 1oz)

Bottom Tier: 1.14kg (2^1/$_2$lb)

Sugarpaste

Colour: Red

Top Tier: 570g (1^1/$_4$lb)

Middle Tier: 950g (2lb 1oz)

Bottom Tier: 1.14kg (2^1/$_2$lb)

Royal Icing

Cream coloured

Ribbons

15mm gold and 1.5mm thin gold braid

Pillars/Separators

3 x 18cm (7") Wilton Harvest Cherub separator set (sprayed gold)

Colours

SK Paste Food Colour: Berberis (use a hint to give cream)

Piping Nozzles

No.1

SILK
FLOWERS

SILVIA
REQUIREMENTS

Flowers/Leaves
All Tiers
Assorted silk flowers and leaves

Cake
Top Tier: 15cm (6") Round
Upper Middle Tier: 20cm (8") Round
Lower Middle Tier: 25cm (10") Round
Bottom Tier: 30cm (12") Round

Boards
Top Tier: 20cm (8") Round drum
Upper Middle Tier: 25cm (10") Round drum
Lower Middle Tier: 30cm (12") Round drum
Bottom Tier: 40cm (16") Round drum

Marzipan
Top Tier: 340g ($^3/_4$lb)
Upper Middle Tier: 570g ($1^1/_4$lb)
Lower Middle Tier: 950g (2lb 1oz)
Bottom Tier: 1.14kg ($2^1/_2$lb)

Sugarpaste
Colour: White
Top Tier: 340g ($^3/_4$lb)

Upper Middle Tier: 570g ($1^1/_4$lb)
Lower Middle Tier: 950g (2lb 1oz)
Bottom Tier: 1.14kg ($2^1/_2$lb)

Royal Icing
White

Ribbons
15mm silver braid

Pillars/Separators
3 x 7.5cm (3") depth round perspex
separator set

Colours
SK Metallic Lustre Dust: Silver

Piping Nozzles
No. 1

BRYONY

REQUIREMENTS

Flowers/Leaves
All Tiers
Assorted silk flowers and leaves

Cake
Top Tier: 15cm (6") Round
Middle Tier: 20cm (8") Round
Bottom Tier: 25cm (10") Round

Boards
Top Tier: 20cm (8") Round drum
Middle Tier: 25cm (10") Round drum
Bottom Tier: 36cm (14") Round drum

Marzipan
Top Tier: 340g ($^3/_4$lb)
Middle Tier: 570g ($1^1/_4$lb)
Bottom Tier: 950g (2lb 1oz)

Sugarpaste
Colour: White & black
Top Tier: 340g ($^3/_4$lb) (white)

Middle Tier: 570g ($1^1/_4$lb) (black)
Bottom Tier: 950g (2lb 1oz)

Royal Icing
White & black coloured

Ribbons
15mm black and white braid

Pillars/Separators
3-tier chrome step stand

Colours
SK Paste Food Colour: Black Extra
Concentrate

Piping Nozzles
No. 1.5

TEGAN

REQUIREMENTS

Flowers/Leaves
All Tiers
Assorted silk flowers and ornamental wood

Cake
Top Tier: 20cm (8") Round
Middle Tier: 25cm (10") Round
Bottom Tier: 30cm (12") Round

Boards
Top Tier: 25cm (10") Round drum
Middle Tier: 30cm (12") Round drum
Bottom Tier: 40cm (16") Round drum

Marzipan
Top Tier: 570g (1$\frac{1}{4}$lb)
Middle Tier: 950g (2lb 1oz)
Bottom Tier: 1.14kg (2$\frac{1}{2}$lb)

Sugarpaste
Demerara
Top Tier: 570g (1$\frac{1}{4}$lb)
Middle Tier: 950g (2lb 1oz)
Bottom Tier: 1.14kg (2$\frac{1}{2}$lb)

Royal Icing
Black coloured

Ribbons
15mm orange

Pillars/Separators
2 x perspex separators
(covered with fabric)

Colours
SK Paste Food Colours: Berberis and Black Extra Concentrate

Piping Nozzles
No. 1

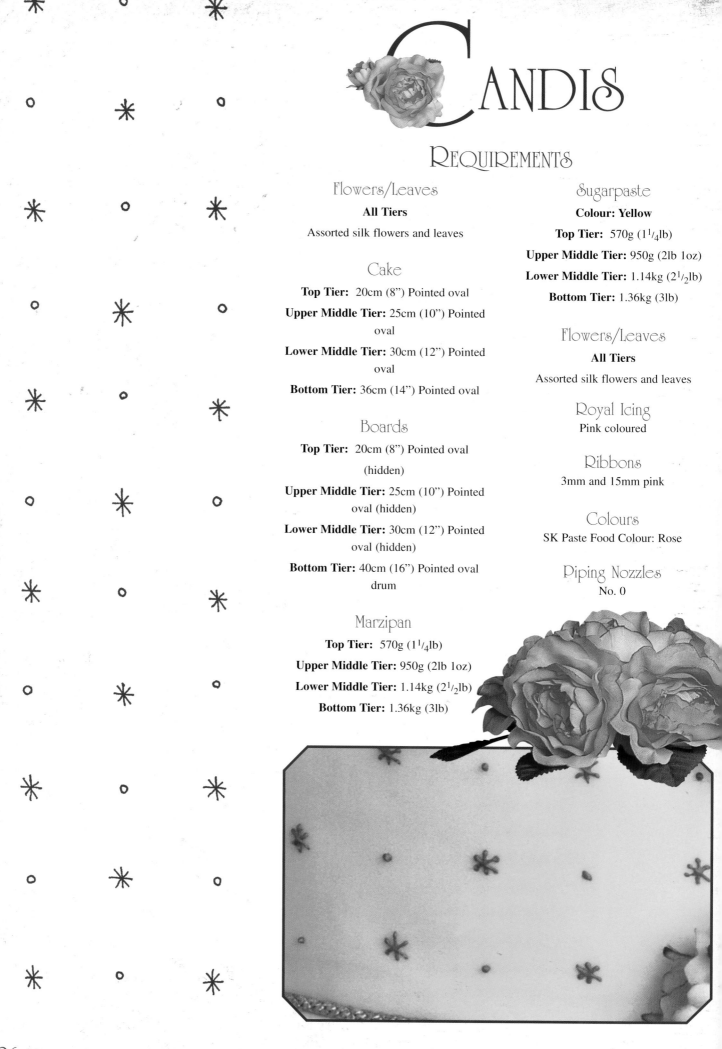

CANDIS

REQUIREMENTS

Flowers/Leaves

All Tiers

Assorted silk flowers and leaves

Cake

Top Tier: 20cm (8") Pointed oval

Upper Middle Tier: 25cm (10") Pointed oval

Lower Middle Tier: 30cm (12") Pointed oval

Bottom Tier: 36cm (14") Pointed oval

Boards

Top Tier: 20cm (8") Pointed oval (hidden)

Upper Middle Tier: 25cm (10") Pointed oval (hidden)

Lower Middle Tier: 30cm (12") Pointed oval (hidden)

Bottom Tier: 40cm (16") Pointed oval drum

Marzipan

Top Tier: 570g (1^1/$_4$lb)

Upper Middle Tier: 950g (2lb 1oz)

Lower Middle Tier: 1.14kg (2^1/$_2$lb)

Bottom Tier: 1.36kg (3lb)

Sugarpaste

Colour: Yellow

Top Tier: 570g (1^1/$_4$lb)

Upper Middle Tier: 950g (2lb 1oz)

Lower Middle Tier: 1.14kg (2^1/$_2$lb)

Bottom Tier: 1.36kg (3lb)

Flowers/Leaves

All Tiers

Assorted silk flowers and leaves

Royal Icing

Pink coloured

Ribbons

3mm and 15mm pink

Colours

SK Paste Food Colour: Rose

Piping Nozzles

No. 0

SHEENA

REQUIREMENTS

Flowers/Leaves

All Tiers

Assorted silk flowers and leaves

Cake

Top Tier: 20cm (8") Heart

Bottom Tier: 30cm (12") Heart

Boards

Top Tier: 25cm (10") Heart drum

Bottom Tier: 40cm (16") Heart drum

Marzipan

Top Tier: 570g (1$\frac{1}{4}$lb)

Bottom Tier: 1.14kg (2$\frac{1}{2}$lb)

Sugarpaste

Colour: Demerara

Top Tier: 570g (1$\frac{1}{4}$lb)

Bottom Tier: 1.14kg (2$\frac{1}{2}$lb)

Royal Icing

Demerara

Ribbons

15mm antique blue and 3mm 3-coloured plait

Pillars/Separators

2-tier chrome "C" stand

Colours

SK Paste Food Colour: Berberis (use a hint to give ivory)

Piping Nozzles

Nos. 0 and 1

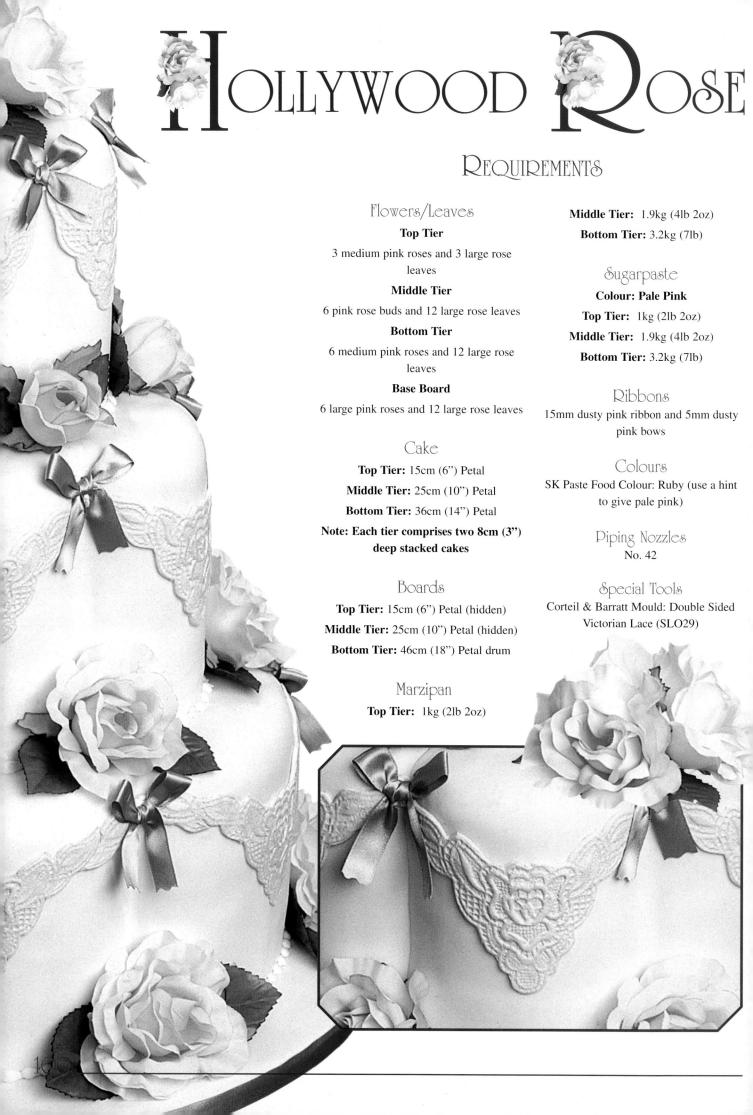

HOLLYWOOD ROSE

REQUIREMENTS

Flowers/Leaves

Top Tier

3 medium pink roses and 3 large rose leaves

Middle Tier

6 pink rose buds and 12 large rose leaves

Bottom Tier

6 medium pink roses and 12 large rose leaves

Base Board

6 large pink roses and 12 large rose leaves

Cake

Top Tier: 15cm (6") Petal

Middle Tier: 25cm (10") Petal

Bottom Tier: 36cm (14") Petal

Note: Each tier comprises two 8cm (3") deep stacked cakes

Boards

Top Tier: 15cm (6") Petal (hidden)

Middle Tier: 25cm (10") Petal (hidden)

Bottom Tier: 46cm (18") Petal drum

Marzipan

Top Tier: 1kg (2lb 2oz)

Middle Tier: 1.9kg (4lb 2oz)

Bottom Tier: 3.2kg (7lb)

Sugarpaste

Colour: Pale Pink

Top Tier: 1kg (2lb 2oz)

Middle Tier: 1.9kg (4lb 2oz)

Bottom Tier: 3.2kg (7lb)

Ribbons

15mm dusty pink ribbon and 5mm dusty pink bows

Colours

SK Paste Food Colour: Ruby (use a hint to give pale pink)

Piping Nozzles

No. 42

Special Tools

Corteil & Barratt Mould: Double Sided Victorian Lace (SLO29)

EDITH

Flowers/Leaves
All Tiers
Assorted silk grapes and leaves

Cake
Top Tier: 15cm (6") Round
Middle Tier: 20cm (8") Round
Bottom Tier: 25cm (10") Round

Boards
Top Tier: 15cm (6") Round (hidden)
Middle Tier: 20cm (8") Round (hidden)
Bottom Tier: 36cm (14") Round drum

Marzipan
Top Tier: 340g ($^3/_4$lb)
Middle Tier: 570g ($1^1/_4$lb)
Bottom Tier: 950g (2lb 1oz)

Sugarpaste
Colour: White
Top Tier: 340g ($^3/_4$lb)
Middle Tier: 570g ($1^1/_4$lb)
Bottom Tier: 950g (2lb 1oz)

Ribbons
15mm thistle

REQUIREMENTS

Flowers/Leaves

Top Tier

6 silk Cosmos flowers and 3 buds

Cake

Top Tier: 15cm (6") Round
Bottom Tier: 25cm (10") Round

Boards

Top Tier: 15cm (6") Round (hidden)
Bottom Tier: 36cm (14") Round drum

Marzipan

Top Tier: 340g ($^3/_4$lb)
Bottom Tier: 950g (2lb 1oz)

Sugarpaste

Colour: White
Top Tier: 340g ($^3/_4$lb)
Bottom Tier: 950g (2lb 1oz)

Royal Icing

White

Ribbons

15mm green and green braid

Piping Nozzles

No. 42

Special Tools

CEP: Oyster Shell mould

SHELBY

FRESH FLOWERS

URSULA

Requirements

Flowers/Leaves

All Tiers

Sprays of white Wendy spray roses set against Tanacetum, Hydrangea, Pittosporum, and Santolina

Cake

Top Tier: 15cm (6") Round

Middle Tier: 20cm (8") Round

Bottom Tier: 25cm (10") Round

Boards

Top Tier: 20cm (8") Round drum

Middle Tier: 25cm (10") Round drum

Bottom Tier: 36cm (14") Round drum

Marzipan

Top Tier: 340g ($^3/_4$lb)

Middle Tier: 570g ($1^1/_4$lb)

Bottom Tier: 950g (2lb 1oz)

Sugarpaste

Colour: White

Top Tier: 340g ($^3/_4$lb)

Middle Tier: 570g ($1^1/_4$lb)

Bottom Tier: 950g (2lb 1oz)

Royal Icing

White

Ribbons

15mm white

Pillars/Separators

13cm (5") and 18cm (7") silver separators

Piping Nozzles

No. 1

**To complete the
design fill in by
piping freehand**

NADINE

REQUIREMENTS

Flowers/Leaves

Top Tier

Champagne roses set against small sprigs
of Genista and Freesias

Bottom Tier

Champagne roses set against small sprigs
of Genista and Freesias

Cake

Top Tier: 20cm (8") Round

Bottom Tier: 30cm (12") Round

Boards

Top Tier: 25cm (10") Round drum

Bottom Tier: 40cm (16") Round drum

Marzipan

Top Tier: 570g (1$^1/_4$lb)

Bottom Tier: 1.14kg (2$^1/_2$lb)

Sugarpaste

Demerara

Top Tier: 570g (1$^1/_4$lb)

Bottom Tier: 1.14kg (2$^1/_2$lb)

Royal Icing

Demerara

Ribbons

15mm gold

Pillars/Separators

2-tier chrome "C" stand

Piping Nozzles

Nos. 0 and 1

NIAMH

REQUIREMENTS

Flowers/Leaves
1 spray comprising snowdrops, Muscari, Mimosa, and cherry blossom

Cake
3 x 20cm (8") Heart

Boards
3 x 23cm (9") Heart

Marzipan
680g (1½lb) per cake

Sugarpaste
Colour: White
680g (1½lb) per cake

Royal Icing
White

Ribbons
Moss green braid (for edge of base boards)

Pillars/Separators
Brass candlestick

Colours
SK Sugar Florist Paste: Holly/Ivy

Piping Nozzles
No. 0

Special Tools
Kemper tool: heart plunger cutter (you will need approximately 400 tiny hearts for each cake)

AMY

REQUIREMENTS

Flowers/Leaves

All Tiers

1 large and 1 small spray comprising Ageratum, Larkspur, Freesias, and Santolina

Cake

Top Tier: 20cm (8") Oval

Bottom Tier: 30cm (12") Oval

Boards

Top Tier: 25cm (10") Oval drum

Bottom Tier: 40cm (16") Oval drum

Marzipan

Top Tier: 570g (1^1/$_4$lb)

Bottom Tier: 1.14kg (2^1/$_2$lb)

Sugarpaste

Colour: White

Top Tier: 570g (1^1/$_4$lb)

Bottom Tier: 1.14kg (2^1/$_2$lb)

Royal Icing

White

Ribbons

15mm white, 15mm silver and 3mm silver

Pillars/Separators

SK Acanthus oval silver separator

Piping Nozzles

No. 1

BERNADETTE

REQUIREMENTS

Flowers/Leaves

All Tiers

Anthurium set against China Grass and Ammi

Cake

Top Tier: 15cm (6") Pointed oval

Middle Top: 20cm (8") Pointed oval

Middle Bottom: 25cm (10") Pointed oval

Bottom Tier: 30cm (12") Pointed oval

Boards

Top Tier: 20cm (8") Pointed oval drum

Middle Top: 25cm (10") Pointed oval drum

Middle Bottom: 30cm (12") Pointed oval drum

Bottom Tier: 40cm (16") Pointed oval drum

Marzipan

Top Tier: 450g (1lb)

Upper Middle Tier: 570g (1$\frac{1}{4}$lb)

Lower Middle Tier: 950g (2lb 1oz)

Bottom Tier: 1.14kg (2$\frac{1}{2}$lb)

Sugarpaste

Colour: Bordeaux (demerara)

Top Tier: 450g (1lb)

Upper Middle Tier: 570g (1$\frac{1}{4}$lb)

Lower Middle Tier: 950g (2lb 1oz)

Bottom Tier: 1.14kg (2$\frac{1}{2}$lb)

Royal Icing

White

Ribbons

15mm white

Pillars/Separators

4-tier chrome cake stand

Colours

SK Paste Food Colour: Bordeaux

Piping Nozzles

Nos. 1 and 2

MARCIA

REQUIREMENTS

Flowers/Leaves

4 clusters comprising lily-of-the-valley,
Esther roses, Freesias, Fritillaria Meleagris,
and Pittosporum

Cake

36cm (14") Round

Boards

50cm (20") Round drum

Marzipan

1.36kg (3lb)

Sugarpaste

Colour: Very pale pink
1.36kg (3lb)

Ribbons

15mm pink

Colours

SK Paste Food Colour: Ruby

REQUIREMENTS

Flowers/Leaves

All Tiers

Sprays comprising Brodiaea, Delphinium
Bluebells, Perris and grey Hebe

Cake

Top Tier: 13cm (5") Square

Middle Tier: 18cm (7") Square

Bottom Tier: 30cm (12") Square

Boards

Top Tier: 13cm (5") Square (hidden)

Middle Tier: 18cm (7") Square (hidden)

Bottom Tier: 40cm (16") Square drum

Marzipan

Top Tier: 260g (9oz)

Middle Tier: 570g ($1^1/_4$lb)

Bottom Tier: 1.14kg ($2^1/_2$lb)

Sugarpaste

Colour: Blue

Top Tier: 260g (9oz)

Middle Tier: 570g ($1^1/_4$lb)

Bottom Tier: 1.14kg ($2^1/_2$lb)

Ribbons

15mm white

Colours

SK Paste Food Colour: Bluebell

CHOCOLATE CAKES

BRONWEN

REQUIREMENTS

Flowers/Leaves
All Tiers
8 orange arum lilies set against autumnal leaves and sprigs of gypsophila

Chocolate Cake
Top Tier: 20cm (8") Oval
Middle Tier: 25cm (10") Oval
Bottom Tier: 30cm (12") Oval

Boards
Top Tier: 20cm (8") Oval (hidden)
Middle Tier: 25cm (10") Oval (hidden)
Bottom Tier: 40cm (16") Oval Drum

Chocolate Marzipan
Dark (see page 9)
Top Tier: 340g ($^3/_4$lb)
Middle Tier: 570g ($1^1/_4$lb)
Bottom Tier: 950g (2lb 1oz)

Covering
All Tiers
500g (1lb 2oz) melted dark couverture

Ribbons
15mm dark brown and 40mm gold/orange ribbon

Colours
SK Metallic Lustre Dust: Light Gold

CHRISSIE

REQUIREMENTS

Flowers/Leaves
All Tiers

Medium and large red roses and buds set against single and sprays of rose leaves, and sprigs of Jubilee Gypsophila

Chocolate Cake
Top Tier: 15cm (6") Round
Middle Tier: 20cm (8") Round
Bottom Tier: 25cm (10") Round

Boards
Top Tier: 15cm (6") Round (hidden)
Middle Tier: 20cm (8") Round (hidden)
Bottom Tier: 36cm (14") Round drum

Chocolate Marzipan
White (see page 9)
Top Tier: 340g ($^3/_4$lb)
Middle Tier: 570g (1$^1/_4$lb)
Bottom Tier: 950g (2lb 1oz)

Covering
All Tiers

300g (11oz) melted white couverture (to adhere chocolate curls)

Decoration
All Tiers

600g box of white chocolate curls

Ribbons
15mm Red

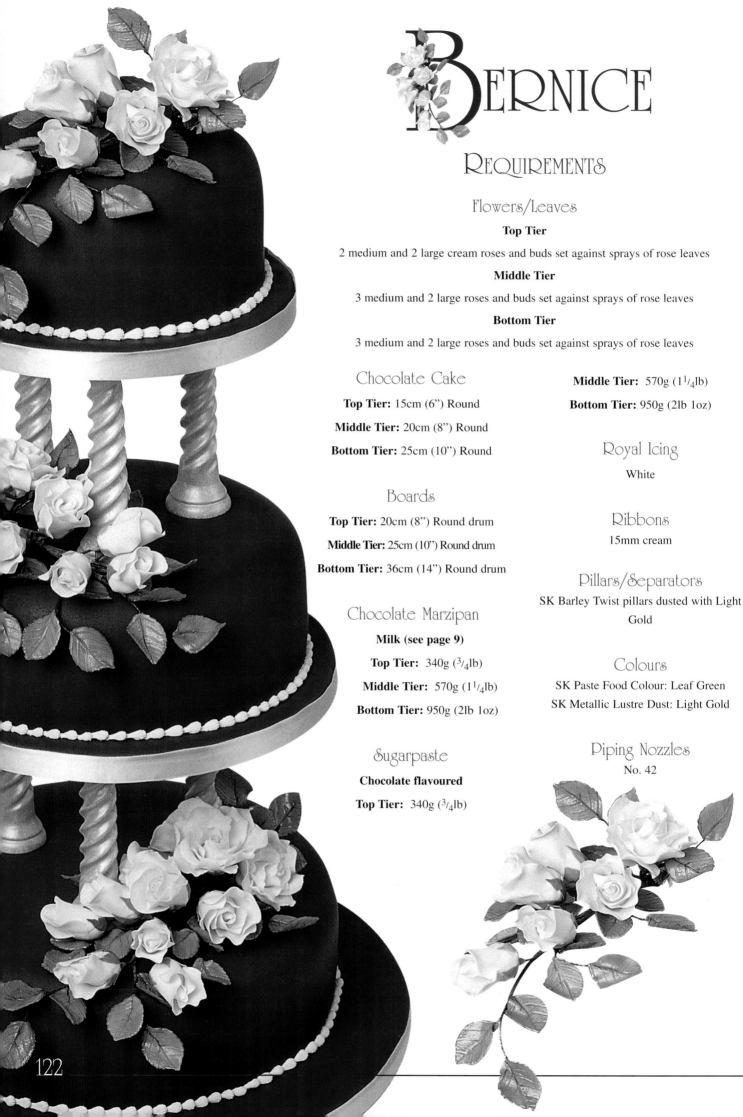

BERNICE

REQUIREMENTS

Flowers/Leaves

Top Tier

2 medium and 2 large cream roses and buds set against sprays of rose leaves

Middle Tier

3 medium and 2 large roses and buds set against sprays of rose leaves

Bottom Tier

3 medium and 2 large roses and buds set against sprays of rose leaves

Chocolate Cake

Top Tier: 15cm (6") Round

Middle Tier: 20cm (8") Round

Bottom Tier: 25cm (10") Round

Boards

Top Tier: 20cm (8") Round drum

Middle Tier: 25cm (10") Round drum

Bottom Tier: 36cm (14") Round drum

Chocolate Marzipan

Milk (see page 9)

Top Tier: 340g ($^3/_4$lb)

Middle Tier: 570g (1$^1/_4$lb)

Bottom Tier: 950g (2lb 1oz)

Sugarpaste

Chocolate flavoured

Top Tier: 340g ($^3/_4$lb)

Middle Tier: 570g (1$^1/_4$lb)

Bottom Tier: 950g (2lb 1oz)

Royal Icing

White

Ribbons

15mm cream

Pillars/Separators

SK Barley Twist pillars dusted with Light Gold

Colours

SK Paste Food Colour: Leaf Green

SK Metallic Lustre Dust: Light Gold

Piping Nozzles

No. 42

CARLA

REQUIREMENTS

Flowers/Leaves
All Tiers
Assorted silk flowers and leaves

Chocolate Cake
Top Tier: 15cm (6") Round
Middle Tier: 20cm (8") Round
Bottom Tier: 25cm (10") Round

Boards
Top Tier: 15cm (6") Round (hidden)
Middle Tier: 20cm (8") Round (hidden)
Bottom Tier: 36cm (14") Round Drum

Chocolate Marzipan
Dark (see page 9)
Top Tier: 340g (³/₄lb)
Middle Tier: 570g (1¹/₄lb)
Bottom Tier: 950g (2lb 1oz)

Sugarpaste
Chocolate flavoured
Top Tier: 340g (³/₄lb)
Middle Tier: 570g (1¹/₄lb)
Bottom Tier: 950g (2lb 1oz)

Decoration
Chocolate shells
Note: Set all three tiers to the back of the
board, leaving room to display flowers and
shells towards the front.

Ribbons
15mm Pink

DOMINIQUE

REQUIREMENTS

Chocolate Cake

Top Tier: 15cm (6") Hexagonal

Upper Middle Tier: 20cm (8") Hexagonal

Middle Tier: 25cm (10") Hexagonal

Lower Middle Tier: 30cm (12") Hexagonal

Bottom Tier: 36cm (14") Hexagonal

Boards

Top Tier: 15cm (6") Hexagonal (hidden)

Upper Middle Tier: 20cm (8") Hexagonal (hidden)

Middle Tier: 25cm (10") Hexagonal (hidden)

Lower Middle Tier: 30cm (12") Hexagonal (hidden)

Bottom Tier: 40cm (16") Hexagonal drum

Chocolate Marzipan

Milk (see page 9)

Top Tier: 500g (1lb 1oz)

Upper Middle Tier: 800g (1³/₄lb)

Middle Tier: 1.02kg (2¹/₄lb)

Lower Middle Tier: 1.14kg (2¹/₂lb)

Bottom Tier: 1.36kg (3lb)

Covering

All Tiers

1kg (2lb 3oz) melted dark couverture

Decoration

300g (1lb 7oz) white chocolate curls

Ribbons

15mm mauve

Colours

SK Moonbeams Iridescent Dust: Sapphire

EMILY

REQUIREMENTS

Flowers/Leaves

Top Tier

3 pink day lilies set against ivory roses, ivory sweet peas, cream Freesias, sprays of eucalyptus leaves, plain leaves, and clusters of green berries

Bottom Tier

5 day lilies set against ivory roses, ivory sweet peas, cream Freesias, sprays of eucalyptus leaves, plain leaves, and clusters of green berries

Chocolate Cake

Top Tier: 20cm (8") Oval

Bottom Tier: 30cm (12") Oval

Boards

Top Tier: 25cm (10") Oval drum

Bottom Tier: 40cm (16") Oval drum

Chocolate Marzipan

Milk (see page 9)

Top Tier: 570g (1^1/$_4$lb)

Bottom Tier: 1.14kg (2^1/$_2$lb)

Covering

All Tiers

400g (14oz) melted milk chocolate couverture

Ribbons

15mm blue and 15mm green

Pillars/Separators

Aqua green candlestick holder

Colours

SK Bridal Satin Lustre Dust: Chiffon Pink

MOLLY

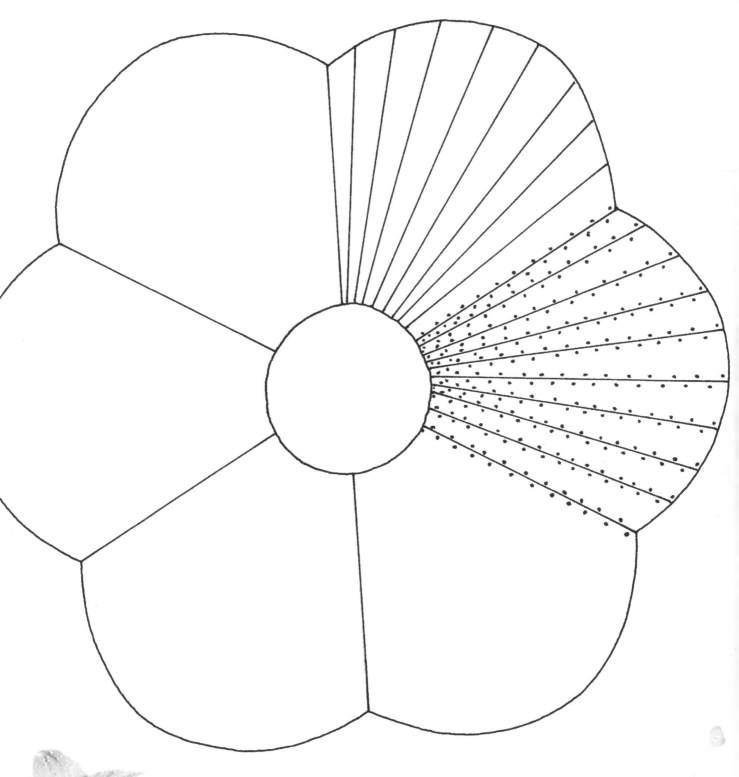

Top design template (refer to pages 82-83)

SUPPLIERS

Manufacturers and Distributors

Culpitt Cake Art
Jubilee Industrial Estate
Ashington
Northumberland
NE63 8UQ
Tel: 01670 814545
Manufacturers and wholesale suppliers of cake decorating and sugarcraft equipment and decorations.

FMM
Unit 5
Kings Park Industrial Estate
Primrose Hill
Kings Langley
Hertfordshire
WD4 8ST
Tel: 01923 268699
Manufacturers and suppliers of cake artistry, bakery and catering equipment.

Great Impressions
Greenlea
14 Studley Drive
Swarlend
Morpeth
Norhumberland
NE65 9JT
Tel: 01670 787061
Manufacturers of veiners (a speciality), moulds and transfers. Mail order.

Guy, Paul & Co.
Unit B4
Foundry Way
Little End Road
Eaton Socon
Cambridgeshire
PE19 3JH
Tel: 01480 472545
Trade suppliers of tools and materials for the art of bakery, sugarcraft and food decoration.

Holly Products
Holly Cottage
Hassall Green
Sandbach
Cheshire
CW11 4YA
Tel: 01270 761403
Moulds, embossers, patterns and tools. Mail order.

PME Sugarcraft
Brember Road
South Harrow
HA2 8UN
Tel: 020 8864 0888
Manufacturers of cake decorating equipment.

Squires Kitchen (Squires Group)
+44 (0)1252 711749
Manufacturer of specialist sugars and food colourings.

Shops

Confectionery Supplies
Unit 11
Foley Trading Estate
Hereford
HR1 2SF
Tel: 01432 371451
Shop, school and trade supplier.

Corteil & Barratt
40 High Street
Ewell Village
Surrey
KT17 1RW
Tel: 020 8393 0032
Shop and school.

Home & Kitchen
7 Victoria Square
Skipton
North Yorkshire
BD23 1JF

Orchard Products
51 Hallyburton Road
Hove
East Sussex
BN3 7GP
Tel: 01273 419418
Manufacturers and suppliers of fine quality sugarcraft cutters and tools. Shop and mail order.

Squires Kitchen Sugarcraft
Squires House
3 Waverley Lane
Farnham
Surrey
GU9 8BB
Tel: 01252 711749
Sugarcraft colours, tools, equipment, silver separators, couverture, marzipans and sugarpastes. Shop, school and mail order.

Publications

Squires Kitchen Magazine Publishing Ltd.
Alfred House
Hones Business Park
Farnham
Surrey
GU9 8BB
Tel: 01252 727572
Publishers of CAKES & Sugarcraft Magazine and WEDDING Cakes - A Design Source Magazine.

Merehurst (an imprint of Murdoch Books UK)
51-57 Lacy Road
Putney
London
SW15 1PR
Tel: 020 8355 1480
Publishers of many cake decorating and sugarcraft titles.

Societies

The British Sugarcraft Guild
Wellington House
Messeter Place
Eltham
London
SE9 5DP
Tel: 020 8859 6943

National Sugarart Association
16 Ridgeway
Hayes
Kent
BR2 7DE
Tel: 020 8777 4445

Florist

Constance Spry
Moor Park House
Moor Park Lane
Farnham
Surrey
GU9 8EN
Tel: 01252 734477
Leading florist and provider of leisure and professional flower arranging and floristry courses.